T0114572

LET'S TALK GOAT... OF
BASKETBALL

MATT PETERS

authorHOUSE®

AuthorHouse™
1663 Liberty Drive
Bloomington, IN 47403
www.authorhouse.com
Phone: 833-262-8899

Published by AuthorHouse 01/29/2021

ISBN: 978-1-6655-1426-2 (sc)
ISBN: 978-1-6655-1429-3 (e)

Library of Congress Control Number: 2021901231

Print information available on the last page.

This book is dedicated to my grandparents and my uncle Fred. I miss them every day.

This book is also dedicated to my children,

My Mom and Dad,

My sister, and my wife.

All of you have stood by me and inspire me.

Thank you all for your support.

Also a special Thank you to the NBA athletes from the past and present.

Table of Contents

TOPICS

The 2020 Los Angeles Lakers are champions, tied with the Boston Celtics for a franchise record most championships with 17 titles. This was an historic accomplishment for not just the franchise, but the players and its fans. People were going crazy online. Twitter was blowing up. Instagram was getting one post after another. I am working the night shift, where it doesn't matter, nor does what I do for a living. I log into YouTube and watch as someone posts a live feed of one of the popular Sports TV talk shows as it's starting. Have you ever looked or participated in the live chats?

On this particular morning, I'm viewing the comments made by fans. I have said in the past, that LeBron James will not get respect and it's his own fans that cause this. They have to disrespect the players who could claim title as the GOAT away from LeBron. As he holds his 4th title and 4th finals MVP, he is ranked by many as the second greatest player to have ever stepped onto the basketball court. He makes a comment about wanting his respect. To be named second greatest ever is not disrespect, that's an accomplishment that most normal people would be happy with. In fact if you watch FS1 or ESPN shows, all of the TV hosts will start with "LeBron is great...." Then they will make whatever point they are trying to make. But every time they make sure to say "LeBron is great." Isn't that giving him respect? Why not just go straight to their point? I have never seen an athlete that is ranked as the best player in the world has such an ego that he has to be called the best by main stream media outlets every time they start to talk about him. Is LeBron James the GOAT? Who is the GOAT if it's not LeBron? Is it Michael Jordan?

First before we can crown him, or anyone else as the GOAT, let's lay the ground rules for what makes the greatest of all time. On October 14, 2020 on the ESPN show Jalen and Jacoby; Jalen Rose listed his criteria by having certain fields that must be met. He listed *NBA titles, Scoring Titles, Most Valuable Player Award (MVP), Finals MVP* and *Defensive Player of the Year.* We will look at These 5 categories and see if those are met in the player's summary. I am also adding Rookie of the year, All Star and All Star MVP as additional criteria. In Every player summary I will list what put them in the GOAT conversation and what is also used against each player.

I do not mean any disrespect to any players I bring up during these debates. Any short comings do not necessarily fall on the individual player. But I will discuss each player and break down some arguments that are common on sports talk shows and in the online community. Also I don't want you to think when I compare LeBron and Jordan that I'm ripping LeBron or Jordan. I am just evening the playing field so both are judged in the same light. Too often both players are attacked by TV hosts and these different topics are not applied to both players. So I took the time to compare these topics to both players. When comparing the all time great players no one needs to be disrespectful of players you believe are not the GOAT.

I brought up disrespect up because the whole argument used for players by fans and media show hosts seem to attack the players they want to say isn't the GOAT. They are quick to try and discredit the GOAT threats to LeBron James. Mainly millennial's are the ones defending their generations' greatest player LeBron James. People who are over 40 tend to put Michael Jordan as their generations greatest player. Before Michael Jordan, there is Magic Johnson, Larry Bird, Kareem Abdul-Jabbar, Wilt Chamberlain and Bill Russell to name a few. Each generation defends their greatest player they saw growing up. That's just natural, why?

It's because that's what we as individuals witnessed as it was happening. It's not the same to watch old matches, games, when we already know the outcome. You are already told who won that game, who was MVP, and who was the champion. It's different when we watch a game live, especially in person.

The atmosphere in a live sporting event is awe inspiring. You see thousands of people in attendance, wearing their team's jerseys, rooting with complete strangers, high fiving when things go right for their teams. The food, music, interaction from mascots and cheerleaders, the experience is just incredible. I would see people of completely different races all getting along as they cheered with each other as their teams played. I enjoyed attending live games in basketball, baseball and football. I never got a chance growing up to go to a Chicago Bulls game, I wish I did. Instead I went to lower level games like the local High schools and colleges. I later moved and starting living in southern California. I used to work in the stadiums, like Qualcomm Stadium back when it had the San Diego Chargers and Petco Park with the San Diego Padres. Being in those environments as fans and eventually as a worker is something I will always cherish and enjoy.

As a child, I didn't go to those stadiums; instead I was in the Midwest outside of Chicago. I got to watch the Chicago White Sox play several times. I eventually lived in Alabama where they have no professional teams. Instead I would travel to Atlanta with my dad were we got to go see the Atlanta Falcons play. I only went when the Cowboys were in town cause dem Boys....they are my team.

When you are at these games and you see your favorite players doing what they do best, it makes you as a kid want to play the sport with them. Kids often pretend they are on that team with their favorite players. As I have grown up, I stopped playing sports until I had kids. Teaching them how to play various sports is so enjoyable to me. It makes me wish I never stopped playing sports, in a way... it makes me jealous of the professional athletes who entertain us every day.

I love to talk sports, even if I don't completely follow it like some people do for their careers. Like many others I turn to the internet and YouTube for my sports entertainment. So of course I watch Fox Sports broadcasts and ESPN shows. I have my favorites and follow certain people on twitter and FaceBook. ESPN hosts I feel are more objective when talking about sports and players. Fox sports on the other hand... some of these guys are extremely biased. To name a few people that are fun to follow and listen to are Freddy Coleman, Stephen A. Smith, Max Kellerman, Paul Pierce, Kendrick Perkins, Skip Bayless, Shannon Sharpe, Chris Carter, Brandon Marshal, Nick Wright and Jenna Wolfe. If Fox Sports is reading this book, have Jenna give more takes because she knows these sports extremely well and her input is rarely given. Also I do not mean any disrespect to Fox Sport by saying their on air personalities are biased; however, they do bring up LeBron often in many segments when they don't need to. They are often pushing the GOAT James narrative which they have been doing since 2016. Nick Wright for example gets extremely personal when it comes to these debates, and while it was fun to watch earlier, he makes it not enjoyable today. I feel ESPN does better; they tend to get more news that are breaking and appear more objective. They don't always talk about LeBron being the GOAT like I see on Fox Sports.

Going back to these live chats I see LeBron fans chanting various anti-Jordan statements. They blasted the live chat on YouTube with statements like Jordan was 1-9. Jordan never won before he had Scottie Pippen and Phil Jackson. Jordan never made it to 10 finals. How is losing before the finals better than losing the championship? As I continue to watch the live chats I can see everyone posting Lakers are Champions. GOAT James!!! And 4-6 > 6-0. Most of these statements are used to try and discredit Michael Jordan in order to give more praise to LeBron James. Do you agree with these statements? How much context is going into these posts? Are they really serious that an MVP with the most finals loses in the history of the sport is better than a man who never lost a championship and got finals MVP in every championship he was in?

I will take a deep dive into these statements and present an argument for each respective GOAT in the game of basketball. I will say at the end of who could be the GOAT and just because I list certain players, does not mean other players cannot be added to the conversation.

Also it's important to mention that many of these players have different roles, different positions. Kareem Abdul-Jabbar, Shaquille O'Neal, Bill Russell, and Wilt Chamberlain were all centers. LeBron James is a small forward. Kobe Bryant and Michael Jordan are both shooting guards. The forward and center positions do tend to place those players closer to the basket, allowing for more rebounds, blocks and even assists. Those players also tend to have higher shooting percentage due to a majority of their shots being taken within a much closer proximity of the basket. Guards on the other hand stay more on the perimeter, they tend to shoot the three or have a mid range shot. Guards also tend to have defenses that involve more steals and are quicker on their movements.

I also want to point out that the ERA that the player lives in also plays a role on their statistics. During Bill Russell and Wilt Chamberlain era, players were all new to the game; the game didn't allow jumping until Bill Russell started doing it. By the time the 70's and 80 come around the game becomes more physical, players get beat up, thrown on the ground when trying to dunk, and hand checking is permitted. The more physical play is not allowed today. Hand checking is no longer allowed in games and now players are not allowed to be touched. So the physicality of the game from the time Jordan played is not always believed by the younger generation. Many of the plays where Jordan gets knocked to the ground would be considered a flagrant foul. Yet those were not called back in the days when Jordan played. In 1979 the three pointer was introduced and that has since effected the statistics on players points and the outcome of games. Style of play in different eras affects the game, it affects the rules, it affects the outcomes. So please do not think that all of these players have all played under the exact same situations and rules. They have not. The game today is considered to be the most soft in NBA history because now players are not allowed to have physical contact with each other like in years past.

The last important thing to point out is most of these debates are opinion based. I do present facts; however, depending on the individual the facts may or may not influence their opinion on who that person believes is the GOAT. I will present to you facts about each player. I will also be telling you my opinions. Most of the arguments have been originally presented on the FOX Sports programs that include First Things First, Undisputed and the Herd. Like I stated previously FOX pushes more for LeBron on being the GOAT which is why I will be discussing what their hosts' debate. Again I mean no disrespect to Nick Wright, Shannon Sharpe or anyone else, but since this is a main topic on their programs I will be dissecting their debates. EPSN will have the debates on occasions but not nearly as often.

Before I begin I want to give you some honorable mentions

Russell Westbrook: This man is often overlooked in many aspects but he has kept his teams in contention for the past decade. While paired with Kevin Durant, James Harden and Kendrick Perkins, they went to face the Miami Heat in the finals back in 2012. Miami won the championship in 5 games. This was the only time thus far in Westbrook's career to have been in the finals. In his career he's averaged 27.2 points, 7.9 rebounds and 7 assists. He is a 9x All NBA and has one regular season MVP award. He also holds a record of three consecutive seasons of averaging triple doubles. The only other player in history to average a triple double for just one season was Oscar Robinson. LeBron got praise for averaging a triple double for just a month. If Russell Westbrook wins a few championships he could possibly enter the conversation but as of now his teams have failed to deliver a championship. Due to this he gets an honorable mention.

Kevin Durant gets an honorable mention due to him placing daggers in the Cavs in back to back years, beating this generation's greatest player LeBron James. Durant's finals record isn't that impressive but he still has a long career ahead of him if he stays healthy. His finals record is 2-2. He's lost to LeBron's Heat in 2012. Even though he was injured in 2019, his team still lost to the Toronto Raptors. Durant did win championships in 2017 and 2018 getting him finals MVP in back to back finals.

He is currently ranked on the all time scoring list at #31, with 22,940 points. NBA.com predicted that he will probably get to #4 all time once his career is done. He's won a regular season MVP, 10X All Star and 4X scoring champion. If he continues to beat some of the top competitors in the game today and gets some more championships, he definitely could be in the GOAT conversation in several years.

What he has keeping him out of the GOAT conversation is many discredit his championships with the Golden State Warriors because they were already a great team before he got there. Many use the excuse that he went to join a 73 win team to win championships. They also say he needs to win a championship away from the Golden State Warriors.

I say this, he got two championships and no matter what people say... both are legitimate championships. He proved he was the best player by winning Finals MVP in those championships. I'll also throw this out there, it should not be held against Durant on joining the Golden State Warriors when we don't take away championships from LeBron James from when he formed a so called Super-team in Miami.

Hakeem Olajuwon gets an honorable mention because he helped the House Rockets become contenders and champions in the mid 90's. Granted his championships came when Michael Jordan had retired... it still counts. He is the second player in NBA history to have won the regular season MVP and defensive player of the year in the same season back in 1994. The first player ever to do this was Michael Jordan. Hakeem also won the championship and finals MVP in 1994 and 1995. Hakeem was also part of the 1992 Olympic Dream Team where he helped the USA win the Olympics gold medal.

Stephen Curry gets an honorable mention due to him being the most recent player to change the way basketball is played today. The game was played for many years by big men and no team could win a championship without a big. Michael Jordan changed this mindset by him being a guard and the Bulls building around him. With Stephen he took the game further but excelling as a 3 point shooter, a sniper as you will. He also has adapted to the play style of the 1996 Bulls where the team was known to have rapid ball movement allowing teammates to be more involved. He is the first unanimous regular season MVP. He is a three time NBA champion. While he has 2 finals loses, he has won 3 championships in 5 years.

While I could list more players like Dr. J, Tim Duncan, David Robinson, Jerry West, Walt Frazier, James Worthy and many others, I know you as the readers want to hear more about the guys who are in the GOAT conversations and not the honorable mentions.

Now onto the goat debates.

Each player I give you has all accomplished something that no one else in the history of the sport has done. These unique feats help each individual being considered as the GOAT. Each player I will present has some stats and accolades that place these players as all time greats. When discussing GOAT we will nitpick and will look at what is for and against each player.

Wilt Chamberlain

Finals record 2-4.

Basketballreference.com provided the following stats for Wilt Chamberlain.

Regular Season

Games played: 1045

Points: 31,419   Points per game: 30.1

Single game points record 100 points.

Rebounds: 23,924   Rebounds per Game: 22.9

Assists: 4,643   Assists per Game: 4.4

Field Goal %: 54%   Free Throw %: 51.1%

Playoffs

Games played: 160

Points: 3,607   Points per game: 22.5

Rebounds: 3913   Rebounds per game: 24.5

Assists: 673   Assists per game: 4.2

ACCOLADES

LandofBasketball.com gave the following accolades for Wilt Chamberlain.

12X All Star

1960 All Star MVP

2X NBA Champion

1X Finals MVP

11X Rebounding Leader

7X Scoring Leader

7X All NBA First Team

3X All NBA Second Team

2X All Defensive First Team

1X Assists Leader.

Rookie of the Year (1959-1960)

Inductive into the Basketball Hall of Fame (HOF) in 1979.

Wilt Chamberlain played in the NBA for 14 seasons; he was in the playoffs for 13 of those seasons. He wore the Jersey number 13 for all three teams he played for, the Philadelphia Warriors, The San Francisco Warriors and the Los Angeles Lakers. He won two championships with two different teams, the Philadelphia Warriors and the Los Angeles Lakers. Wilt is in the GOAT conversation because he has scoring titles, regular season MVP, finals MVPs and is a 2 time champion. His stats which include him scoring 100 points in a single game have been unmatched in the NBA's history. He still holds records for most points scored in multiple games. He has 32 games in his career where he has scored 60 or more points. In retrospect, Kobe Bryant has 6 such games in his career, Michael Jordan has 4, and LeBron James has 1. The list of the points and games are on nbahoopsonline.com. Wilt has also many statistical records, many of which have withstood the test of time. His statistics put him as one of the top contenders for the GOAT, rivaling that of LeBron James for statistical dominance.

What is used against Wilt is his stats say he was the best player at the time but he could not win and overtake Bill Russell and the Boston Celtics. Due his statistical dominance, he underachieved and should have more championships.

Bill Russell

Finals record: 11-1.

Basketballreference.com gave the following stats for Bill Russell.

Regular season

Games played: 963

Points: 14, 522   Points per Game: 15.1

Rebounds: 21,620   Rebounds per Game: 22.5

Assists: 4,100.   Assists Per Game: 4.3

Field goal %: 44%   Free Throw %: .56.1%

Playoffs Statistics

Games: 165

Points: 2,673   Points per Game: 16.2

Rebounds: 4,104   Rebounds per Game: 24.9

Assists: 770   Assists Per Game: 4.7

Field Goal %: 43%   Free Throw %: 60.3%

ACCOLADES

LandofBasketball.com gave the following accolades for Bill Russell.

11X NBA champion.

12X All Star

1X All Star MVP 1963

5X Regular season MVP

4X Rebounds leader

3X All NBA First Team

8X All NBA Second Team

1X All Defensive Team

Bill Russell is considered the greatest winner in all of the NBA and if you include all sports he still stands alone as the most dominant winner in all sports history.

When he was in college he won back to back college championships and in his last college season won 55 games in a row (HBO documentary *My Life, My Way*). Bill revolutionized the sport by being the first to jump in order to block a shot; before he did that players tried to keep their feet on the floor. This changed how the game of basketball was played. He was known as a team player and it showed by the Boston Celtics making the playoffs for the 13 seasons Bill Russell played for them. He was inducted into the NBA hall of fame in 1975 (Land of Basketball website).

In GOAT debates he wins as the player with the most Championship rings, making him stand alone with 11 championships. He is also the only player to be in the championship nearly every season of his career. He won 8 straight championships in a row from 1959 to 1966. He is the only person to be a coach at the same time he was an active player and win a championship. He made history by being the first black coach in the NBA and is the first black coach to win a championship.

These things are often overlooked when sports analysts talk of the goat debates. He does get recognition as an all star, with regular season MVP awards and his 11 championships. Most of his career history is left out, like Bill Russell beating Wilt Chamberlain in Russell's last championship.

What weakens his goat debate is that he did lose one championship to the St. Louis Hawks in 1958. He never got the finals MVP or the Rookie of the year. Since we do have to nitpick his one lost in the championship is a negative. However that lost came early in his career. He also did not get defensive player of the year, or any scoring titles. For the most part there are not many things that go against him as a player, and he should remain in every goat conversation.

Irvine Magic Johnson

Basketballreference.com and LandofBasketball.com gives the following statistics

Regular Season

Games played: 906

Points: 17, 707 Points per game: 19.5

Rebounds 6,559 Rebounds per game: 7.2

Assists: 10,141 Assists per game: 11.2

Steals: 1,724 Steals per game: 1.9

Blocks: 374 Blocks per game: 0.4

Free Throw %: 84.8

LandofBasketball.com gave the following *playoff statistics.*

Games: 190

Points 3,701   Points per game: 19.5

Rebounds: 1,465   Rebounds per game: 7.7

Assists: 2,346   Assists per game12.3

Steals: 358   Steals per game. 1.9

Blocks: 64   Blocks per game. 0.3

LandofBasketball.com listed his accolades

5X NBA champion

12X ALL star

2X ALL star MVP

3X MVP

3X Finals MVP

4X Assists leader

2X Steals Leader

9X All NBA First team

1X All NBA Second Team

1979-80 Rookie of the Year.

1979-80 ALL rookie First Team.

Finals record 5-4.

Life Time Achievement Award

Magic Johnson was dominant in the 80's. He is easily the best or at the least a top 5 player in the game. He is the only player I found that won Rookie of the year, won a championship and got finals MVP in his rookie campaign back in 1979/80. In his rookie season he helped the Lakers reach the finals where he faced the Philadelphia 76ers who were led by Julius Erving, aka Dr. J. After Kareem got injured in game 5, Magic didn't back down, instead he stepped up and helped the Lakers go on in win the title. He did this as a rookie! He came into the NBA as a winner. If anyone wants to judge a GOAT as winning right as they come into the NBA and is the best player right off the bat, look no further than Magic Johnson. To compare Michael Jordan, LeBron James, Wilt Chamberlain, and Kareem Abdul-Jabbar did not do his in their respective rookie seasons. "The most dominate duo's of all time is Kareem and Magic" Stated Shannon Sharpe on Undisputed on December 17, 2020. While other duos are great and debated on the show, Shannon did point out that together they went to eight finals in the 1980's. During the 1980's Magic Johnson also went to the championship in 80, 82, 83, 84, 85, 87, 88, 89. That's eight finals appearances. The Lakers would win five championships in that span. Magic Johnson's last trip to the championship would be in his final season in 1991 when he would lose to Michael Jordan and the Chicago Bulls. Many wonder if Magic Johnson didn't have to step away from basketball because of him getting sick if he might have gone on to win more.

Off the court he has been in ownership positions where he has helped build difference sport franchises into winning clubs. The LA Dodgers and Sparks have won championships while he has been a owner of those ball clubs. He also helped get the ball rolling as they say for the current LA Lakers run for championships by bringing big time free agent LeBron James to the Lakers in 2018/19 seaon.

What goes against Magic is he never got the defensive player of the year award. He also has 4 losses in the championship. He was just one finals appearance shy of having 10 finals appearances like Kareem and LeBron. He also did not get finals MVP in every championship he was in.

Kareem Abdul-Jabbar

Basketballreference.com provided the following stats for Kareem Abdul-Jabbar.

Regular Season

Games played: 1560.

Points: 38,387   Points per game: 24.6

Rebounds: 17,440   Rebounds per game: 11.2

Assists: 5660   Assists per game: 3.6

Field Goal %: 55.9%   Free Throw %: 72.1%   3FG%: 5.6%

Playoff statistics

Games: 237

Points: 5,762   Points per game: 24.3

Rebounds: 2,481   Rebounds per game: 10.5

Assists: 767   Assists per game: 3.2

Field goal %: 53.3%   Free Throws: 74%

Blocks: 447   Blocks per game: 2.4

Steals: 189   Steals per game: 1.0

LandofBasketball.com provided the following accolades for Kareem Abdul-Jabbar.

19X All Stars (Played in 18 of those ALL star games).

6X champion

6X MVP

2X Finals MVP

2X Scoring Leader

4X Blocks Leader

1X Rebounding Leader

10X ALL NBA First Team

5X All NBA Second Team

5X All Defensive First Team

6X All Defensive Second Team

1969-70 Rookie of the year

1969-70 All Rookie First Team.

NBA finals Record: 6-4.

Presidential Medal of Freedom (2016).

Kareem Abdul-Jabbar is one of the greatest players to ever have played the game. He is the all time scoring leader with 38,387 career points. He had the un-block-able "Sky hook" shot and was able to go to the NBA finals 10 separate times. His finals record is the opposite of where LeBron James is currently. Kareem stands at 6-4; whereas LeBron James is 4-6. In Kareem's Rookie season he was All NBA Second team, All Defensive second team, rookie of the year and all rookie first team.

If the GOAT standard is to have the most career points, having a shot no one could block and have the most regular season MVP awards, then Kareem stands alone. He also has 2 finals MVP awards, 6 championships, and is 2 times scoring leader. He is definitely should be up there in the GOAT debates, but is rarely used in actual debates we see on TV. Often he is not talked about enough as a candidate for GOAT and deserves more respect. Without Kareem there is not likely the Show Time Lakers of the 1980's.

What goes against Kareem is his championship loses, he never got defensive player of the year and people try to say he was part of a Dynasty like it's a bad thing. He was the focal point on the Lakers and they built around him, just like many other big men from the 1980s and 90s. He was so hard to guard that they made dunking illegal which is why the sky hook shot was used by Kareem. Like many others, its hard to say anything bad about Kareem Abdul-Jabbar as a player. He was incredible and like Wilt and Bill, he would be in every GOAT debate.

Larry Bird

The following stats are provided by Basketballreference.com

Career Games: 897.

Points: 21, 791.	Points per game: 24.3
Rebounds: 8, 974	Rebounds per game: 10.0
Assists: 5, 695	Assists per game: 6.3

Blocks: 755

Steals: 1,556

Field Goal %: 49.6%   Three point%: 37.6%   Free Throw %: 88.6%

Playoff statistics:

Games: 164

Points: 3,897	Points per game: 23.8
Rebounds: 1,683	Rebounds per game: 10.3
Assists: 1,062	Assists per game: 6.5
Blocks: 145	Blocks per game: 0.9
Steals: 296	Steals per game: 1.8

Field Goal %: 47.2%   Three Point %: 32.1%   Free Throw %: 89%

NBA.com provided the following accolades for Larry Bird.

15X NBA player of the week.

1X NBA Sporting News Rookie
of the Year.

3X ALL defensive Team

1X Olympic Gold Medal Winner

LandofBasketball.com provided the following accolades for Larry Bird.

3X Champion

12X All Star

1X All Star MVP

3X MVP

2X Finals MVP

9X All NBA First Team

1X All NBA Second Team

1979-80 Rookie of the year.

Finals Record 3-2.

Life Time Achievement Award

    Larry Bird was part of a Celtics dynasty in the 1980's. He and three other HOF players dominated the teams in the Eastern Division beating many great players and teams including Michael Jordan. He played alongside HOF players Dennis Johnson, Robert Parish and Kevin McHale. He also played alongside Danny Ainge who would later become an All Star. This Boston Celtics Dynasty was the original super-team of that time competing against the other dynasty in the Western Division, the Los Angeles Lakers. Larry is definitely in the GOAT conversation due to him being a 3 time champion, he has finals and regular season MVPs, and had rookie of the year. Larry Bird's passing ability was simply amazing, I was too young to have watched him and remember it. I have had to go and look at highlights and re-watch old games to really appreciate what he did. He is arguably one of the best passers to have ever played the game of basketball.

    What Larry Bird lacks is no defensive player of the year, he didn't get any scoring titles and his loses in the finals are a negative. His Boston Celtics were one of four teams to be winning championships from the 1980 to 1990. Other teams include the Los Angeles Lakers, Detroit Pistons and Philadelphia 76ers. This Boston Celtics team made it to the championship 5 times during his career mainly facing the Lakers. This rivalry is one of the best ever in the NBA. Today Larry Bird and Magic Johnson have become best friends and are always giving each other much do respect for their careers.

Shaquille O'Neal

Basketballreference.com provided the following stats for Shaquille O'Neal.

Regular Season statistics

Games: 1207

Points: 28,596   Points per game: 23.7

Rebounds: 13,099   Rebounds per game: 10.9

Assists: 3,026   Assists per game: 2.5

Blocks: 2,732   Blocks per game: 2.3

Steals: 739   Steals per game: 0.6

Field Goal%: 58.2%   Three Point%: 4.5   Free Throw%: 52.7%

Playoff Statistics

Points: 5,250   Points per game: 24.3

Rebounds: 2,508   Rebounds per game: 11.6

Assists: 582   Assists per game: 2.7

Blocks: 459   Blocks per game: 2.1

Steals 117   Steals per game: 0.5

Field Goal %: 56.3%   Three Point %: N/A   Free Throw %: 50.4%

LandofBasketball.com provided the following accolades for Shaquille O'Neal.

Inducted into the basketball Hall of Fame in 2016.

4X Champion

15X All Star

3X All Star MVP

1X MVP

3X Finals MVP

2X Scoring Leader

8X All NBA First Team

2X All NBA Second Team

4X All NBA Third Team

3X All Defensive Team

1992-93 Rookie of the year

All Rookie First Team

Finals record: 4-2.

Shaquille O'Neal came into the NBA as a force to be reckoned with. His size and athleticism is something that is rarely seen in the NBA. He had a dominating presence and is the only big man in recent memory to have received MVP and finals MVP awards. There were three All Star games that he missed all due to injury. He is often given credit by sports analysts and even players that had he stayed focused and stayed in shape he would be the GOAT. Many believed that had he had that drive he could have won many more championships. I do think that had things maybe played out differently in LA, he would have won more championships. The fact that really no player could defend against him is something that the NBA had not seen since Kareem Adbul-Jabbar. Shaq as the GOAT is in the conversation due to these reasons and having the championships, with regular season MVP, finals MVPs along with scoring titles helps his case.

What's used against Shaq is he lacked the discipline to stay in shape and didn't show dedication or desire to win. This is part of the reason we saw the beef between him and Kobe in the early 2000s. He only really lacks defensive player of the year and the 2 finals loses is often forgotten. There is not many negatives that go against Shaq as far as his career will show. During his career, he was a poor free throw shooter so late in the game opposing teams were not afraid to foul him, there was a very good chance he would miss the free throw, giving the opposing team an opportunity to get the rebound then possibly score.

Kobe Bryant

Basketballreference.com provided the following stats for Kobe Bryant.

Regular season games: 1,346

Regular Season

Points: 33,643   Points per game: 25.0

Rebounds: 7,047   Rebounds per game: 5.2

Assists: 6,306   Assists per game: 4.7

Steals: 1,944   Steals per game: 1.4

Blocks: 640   Blocks per game: 0.5

Field goal %: 44.7%   Three Point %: 32.9%   Free Throw %: 83.7%

Playoff Statistics

Points: 5,640   Points per game: 25.6

Rebounds: 1,119   Rebounds per game: 5.1

Assists: 1,040   Assists per game: 4.7

Steals: 310   Steals per game: 1.4

Blocks: 144   Blocks per game: 0.7

Field goal %: 44.8%   Three Point %: 33.1%   Free Throw %: 81.6%

LandofBasketball.com provided the following accolades.

5X Champion

2X Finals MVP

18X All star

4X All Star MVP

1X MVP

2X Scoring leader

11X All NBA First Team

2X All NBA Second Team

9X All Defensive First Team

3X All Defensive Second Team

Kobe was known for his killer instinct often referred to his Black Mamba mentality. He is called Mr. 81 due to him scoring 81 points in a single game in honor of his grandmother who came to watch him play in a live game for the first time (NBA.com). He is one of the most Iconic legends to come out of the Los Angeles Lakers organization. He did not play in 3 all star games due to injuries. He will be in the 2020 hall of fame class with Tim Duncan and Kevin Garnett.

It is unfortunate that in early 2020 he passed away from a tragic helicopter crash just a day after LeBron James passed him on the all time scoring list. Fans of the sport know how important he was to LA and to basketball. Kobe won regular season MVP, All Star MVP, finals MVP, and scoring titles to help place him in the goat conversation. He even got 2 gold medals in the Olympics. Even after his career ended in basketball, he continues to sell shoes and other endorsements. He got an Oscar, Sports Emmy and Annie Award for his film *Dear Basketball* is another accolade that is added to his impressive resume.

Basketball lost a legend, fans and myself included miss seeing him. RIP Kobe.

Before I get into the last two on my GOAT debate I want to take time to say that after listing their stats and accolades, I will break down the separate arguments in the GOAT debates that I often hear. I will give my input but know any argument I give for one will also be applied to the other. I will be answering questions that are applied in these debates and will also give any context that is left out by many sports analysts. I will also refer about the start of the book where I stated its LeBron's fans that cause much of the disrespect he receives. That will be towards the end of my arguments. Without further ado, here are the final two in the greatest of all time in the basketball debates.

LeBron James

Basketballreference.com provided the following statistics for LeBron James.

Regular Season statistics

Games: 1265

Points: 34,241	Points per game: 27.1	
Rebounds: 9,405	Rebounds per game: 7.4	
Assists: 9,346	Assists per game: 7.4	
Steals: 2,015	Steals per game: 1.6	
Blocks: 957	Blocks per game: 0.8	
Field Goal%: 50.4%	Three Point%: 34.4%	Free Throw%: 73.4%

Playoff Statistics

Games:

Points: 7,491	Points per game: 28.8	
Rebounds: 2,348	Rebounds per game: 9.0	
Assists: 1,871	Assists per game: 7.2	
Steals: 445	Steals per game: 1.7	
Blocks: 250	Blocks per game: 1.0	
Field Goal%: 49.6%	Three Point%: 33.5%	Free Throw%: 74.1%

LandofBasketball.com provided the following accolades for LeBron James.

4X Champion

4X Finals MVP

4X MVP

16X ALL star

3X ALL star MVP

1X Scoring Leader

1X Assist Leader

13X All NBA First Team

2X All NBA Second Team

1X All NBA Third Team

5X All Defensive Team

1X All Defensive Second Team

2003-04 Rookie of the Year.

All Rookie First Team.

LeBron as of 2020 has been to ten NBA finals during his 17 year career, making it to where he's spent nearly 59 % of his career in position to win a championship. Most NBA franchises haven't been to the championship as many times like LeBron has.

He holds many statistical accomplishments and records and even broke two of Michael Jordan records of career points scored and most consecutive games of 10 points or more scored. The double digit points scored record is currently at 995 games. He broke Michael Jordan record back in 2018 where Jordan had 866 consecutive double digit point games. LeBron even passed Jordan on the all time points scored list putting James currently in third place while Jordan is at 5th place. LeBron also has 4 championships and 4 finals MVP.

There are four players to have won championships with 3 different ball clubs. Those players to win championships in three different franchises include LeBron James, Robert Horry, John Salley and Danny Green. LeBron is the only player on this list to have gotten Finals MVP with all three ball clubs; the others on this list have not won finals MVP.

The argument against LeBron in the GOAT debates are several things and like Jordan are mainly narrative arguments. He has the meltdown of the 2011 NBA finals vs. the Dallas Mavericks, when LeBron was on a loaded Miami Heat team. He has had super teams in nearly every championship his team has won. In Miami he had Dwayne Wade, Chris Bosh and later Ray Allen. When he went back to Cleveland he had Kyrie Irving and Kevin Love. When he joined the Lakers he missed the playoffs for the third time in his career. In 2019, the Lakers bring in Anthony Davis, a top 5 NBA player to join LeBron. While he has needed help to win, his help that is brought in tends to be players in the top 5 or top 10 in the league, I will talk more about this in the GOAT arguments section. LeBron also lacks on the defensive end of the floor and seems to focus every game on getting his 10+ points, rebounds and assists. Often he is attributed with stat padding, especially in games he knows he will be losing.

With all of the impressive statistics he brings, he has not won as often as he should have. He holds a "Wilt Chamberlain argument" as Chris Broussard has said. LeBron has impressive stats but many short comings in the championships. He is the only MVP [on this list I provided] to have lost 6 championships making it the most by any former MVP.

Michael Jordan

The following statistics are provided by Basketballreference.com on Michael Jordan.

Regular season statistics

Games: 1072

Points: 32,292   Points per game: 30.1

Rebounds: 6,672   Rebounds per game: 6.2

Assists: 5,633   Assists per game: 5.3

Steals: 2,514   Steals per game: 2.3

Blocks: 893   Blocks per game: 0.8

Field Goal%: 49.7 %   Three Point %: 32.7%   Free Throw%: 83.5%

Playoff Statistics

Games: 179

Points: 5987   Points per game: 33.4

Rebounds: 1,152   Rebounds per game: 6.4

Assists: 1022   Assists per game: 5.7

Steals: 376   Steals per game: 2.1

Blocks: 158   Blocks per game: 0.9

Field Goal%: 48.7%   Three Point %: 33.2%   Free Throw%: 82.8%

LandofBasketball.com provided the following accolades for Michael Jordan.

6X Champion

6X Finals MVP

5X MVP

1X Defensive Player of the Year

14X ALL star

3X ALL star MVP

10X Scoring Leader

3X Steals Leader

10X All NBA First Team

1X All NBA Second Team

9X All Defensive First Team

1984-85 Rookie of the Year.

All Rookie First Team.

2X Olympic Gold Medal

2X Slam Dunk Champion

3X Associated Press Athlete of the year (91, 92, and 93)

Sports Illustrated Sportsperson of the year 1991

NBA's 50th Anniversary All Time Team

1982 NCAA Champion

2X Consensus 1st Team All American 83/84

ACC Player of the Year 1984

2X First Team All-ACC 83-84

ACC Rookie of the Year 1982

2X USA Basketball Male Athlete of the Year 83/84

McDonald's Open Championship 1997

Retired 23 with North Carolina Tar heels, Miami Heat and Chicago Bulls.

2016 Presidential Medal of Freedom.

Michael Jordan is often referred to as the GOAT in basketball. Many Analysts say he's the greatest and no other player has won and dominated like he did during his career. If you look at his game he has literally no flaws. He was a great shooter, he didn't shoot the 3 like it's done today but he was still a threat beyond the arch. His three point shots are nearly identical to Kobe Bryant. Chris Broussard has said no one says the three point shot was a weakness of Kobe, so it wasn't a weakness of Jordan's. He broke the record for the most threes made in a single half for an NBA finals game. In the 1992 NBA finals game 1 against the Portland Trailblazers, Jordan made a record with 6 three pointers in the first half. Jordan would go on to say "it was like shooting a free throw really." He was a great free throw shooter averaging over 80% during his career. He could shoot the mid range shot and was a 2 time slam dunk champion. His accolades tell a story of him dominating not just in offense but also in defense. He led the league on steals for three consecutive years. In 1988 he won the regular season MVP awards, ALL star game MVP, scoring title, All NBA first team, all defensive first team and Defensive Player of the Year. Winning all of those awards in the same season was unheard of. He was the first player in history to get MVP and defensive player of the year in the same season.

EPSN Stephen A. Smith, Max Kellerman, and FS1 Undisputed Skip Bayless have pointed out that Michael Jordan never went to a game seven in the finals. They also have pointed out the competition that Jordan and the Bulls faced. What is a surprise is many say Jordan was favored to win every championship he was in. There were only four championships Jordan was favored to win. The championships in 1991, 1992, 1996 and 1997 the Chicago Bulls were favored to win the championship. However in 1993 and 1998 the Bulls were not. This is mainly because there has been a history in the NBA where most teams do no three-peat, especially more than once. Depending on which site you choose to go to, some say Jordan was always expected to win the championship, others put the Jordan lead Bulls as underdogs. Never the Less, the Bulls Won and now history places these Bulls teams on a higher pedestal because of Michael Jordan.

Jordan faced tough competition and the reason it seemed like he didn't is because when he started winning he didn't stop winning. This is all part of Jordan's history, it's in his resume for the GOAT. Michael Jordan has the most complete resume for the GOAT argument. Rather than putting his resume in context right now, I'm going to put it at the very end. So stay tuned.

The arguments against MJ as the goat. Do you remember the statements I referred to at the very beginning of this book? Many of these arguments against MJ I will go over in detail in the next section of the book. What fans and analysts often refer to are narrative arguments. They back it from black and white statistics because, hey, it happened right? Michael Jordan and the Bulls did lose the first round of playoffs from the 1985 to 1987. MJ didn't win without all stars and HOF players next to him. MJ also wasn't a great 3 point shooter but he wasn't poor at it either. MJ left the game twice during the prime if his career. His analytics are not as good as LeBron's. MJ seasons with the Wizards showed he could not lead a team to a championship. And finally MJ did not beat any great teams or players. These are the arguments against him. So how is he still considered the GOAT?

Did I mention I didn't list all of the reasons that go against LeBron? These things are for the debate of the top 2 in the GOAT debates: Michael Jordan VS LeBron James.

THE DEBATE

I often hear many different arguments that are aimed at discrediting great players. The arguments are to boost another star, mainly discredit Michael Jordan to boost LeBron James. These narrative arguments need to be given with proper context because by a fan listening, having no prior knowledge or experience, will just believe what's being told to them. I don't like these arguments because they are too often one sided and if the sports analysts applied these same statements to LeBron it weakens the LeBron argument for the goat status more than it hurts Jordan. Also some arguments to boost Jordan can hurt him as well, because depending on what argument is used and how it's used we now start to bring in the other players I mentioned as potential GOATs.

Argument 01: Jordan could not win without an all star Scottie Pippen and all time great coach Phil Jackson next to him

This argument was brought up by Nick Wright on First things First. He tries to use it to say Michael Jordan was a loser and "got bounced out of the first round for three consecutive years." He also claims that Michael Jordan couldn't win until he got a hall of famer Scottie Pippen and a legendary coach Phil Jackson to join him.

Here is my rebuttal.

Part 1 Jordan needing Pippen

This statement is of Jordan needing another Star like Scottie Pippen is true and it's a narrative argument that hides behind the Bulls records for the first three seasons of Jordan's career. With Jordan not having many negative shortcomings this is one I see LeBron fanatics attack the most. They claim that without Pippen and Jackson he would have never won. That's hypothetical so it loses value in the argument. There's no room for hypothetical arguments. However in the Chicago Bulls documentary The Last Dance Michael Jordan does say "Everybody says well, I won all these championships, but I didn't win without Scottie Pippen. And, you know, that's why I consider him the best teammate of all time." Episode 2 of The LAST dance.

The truth is no star can win without other players around them, example Bill Russell was not the best player in the NBA but he had the better team, and due to this he won 11 championships. Bill also helped the fast pace offense that Boston ran and gave his teammates more opportunities to score, which is why Bob Cousy won finals MVP during that Boston dominant era.

Larry Bird is recognized as one of the all-time greatest players to ever play the game. NBA.com says he is a "scorer, a passer, a rebounder, a defender, a team player, and, perhaps above all, as a clutch performer." He went to the championship on five separate occasions. He helped Boston reach the finals in 4 consecutive seasons from 1984 to 1987. He won 3 championships [1981, 1984, and 1987]. He did this with other great players around him. Larry Bird did not get to the championship 5 times on his own.

Magic Johnson wouldn't have won without James Worthy and Kareem Abdul-Jabbar with him. The ShowTime Lakers domination of the 70s and 80s is due to them having this dynasty. Yet we don't hear about the dominant players of the Lakers as much because that's not the focus, instead the arguments shift to Jordan losing then becoming a winner. What we also hear about is in the 90s with the Chicago Bulls becoming the most dominant Dynasty of that era.

But if we stay focused on the 1980s we get a different narrative of Michael Jordan. Jordan was dominant but couldn't win. In fact, Michael Jordan would not have won the 1982 NCAA championship game without his teammate James Worthy playing with him. After that championship Worthy enters the NBA and plays for the Lakers. Jordan than loses a championship before entering the NBA.

Jordan then was drafted in 1984 to a horrible Chicago Bulls franchise which was a losing team. Fans in Chicago didn't even follow the team; they were fans in the other sports like football, baseball and hockey [Last dance documentary]. Jordan did not win a championship by himself. The truth is he went 7 years before winning his first championship (1985, 1986, 1987, 1988, 1989, 1990). 1991 Jordan won his first championship.

It took LeBron 9 years to win his (2004, 2005, 2006, 2007, 2008, 2009, 2010, 2011 he did not win a championship). 2012 LeBron and the Miami Heat won the championship against the Thunder. This would be LeBron's first championship. I list the years in which the season ends. Keep in mind we don't say the 1990 bulls were champions; we say the 91 Bulls were champions, because that's the actual year the championship occurred. So using this context you can see why I don't start with Jordan in 84 because he did not play the 1983/84 season, he played the 1984/85 season, so 85 is the first playoff listed for his career. James same context, he entered the NBA in 2003. So his first season was 2003/04 season, first playoff was 2004 which his team was not able to participate in, but still counts as he's an active player in the NBA.

Jordan also faced more than one great team outside of the Los Angeles Lakers. The Boston Celtics were a force in the mid 80s. In fact Jordan's main competitors in his early career were the Milwaukee Bucks, Boston Celtics and Detroit Pistons. The Boston Celtics had 4 HOF players with Larry Bird, Robert Parish, Bill Walton and Kevin McHale. During the 80s Lakers and Celtics were battling several times for championships.

The truth is none of these teams would dominate and win with only one great player. It is used against Michael Jordan that he would face the Milwaukee Bucks and Boston Celtics earlier in the playoffs compared to LeBron facing the Golden State Warriors and San Antonio Spurs in the finals. For the most part all great teams that win a championship tend to have more than one great player on the team. It's not LeBron or Jordan's fault on when they faced these great teams.

It is also overlooked that Scottie Pippen was not great when he first came into the League. He didn't reach the all star level until the 1990 season. In 1991 He wasn't an all star that year when Chicago won their first championship.

The chart below shows Scottie Pippen's stats from 88-994.

Season	Games	MP	FG%	3p%	FT%	TRB	AST	STL	PTS
1987-88	79	20.9	.463	.174	.576	3.8	2.1	1.2	7.9
1988-89	73	33.1	.476	.273	.668	6.1	3.5	1.9	14.4

1989-90	82	38.4	.489	.250	.675	6.7	5.4	2.6	16.5
1990-91	82	36.8	.520	.309	.706	7.3	6.2	2.4	17.8
1991-92	82	36.6	.506	.200	.760	7.7	7.0	1.9	21.0
1992-93	72	38.6	.473	.237	.663	7.7	6.3	2.1	18.6
1993-94	72	38.3	.491	.320	.660	8.7	5.6	2.9	22.0

So yes, Jordan needed more stars with him. Scottie Pippen was the first major star that the Bulls acquired to get Michael Jordan help. Keep in mind, Scottie Pippen was a rookie in the 87/88 season. It would take him three years before his first all star appearance in 1990. So Jordan would need players like Scottie Pippen, Horace Grant, BJ Armstrong and Bill Cartwright to win. As Magic Johnson said in the last dance Documentary in Episode 2, "Guy's like myself and Larry who knew the game, who knew championship basketball, we knew the guy was coming. Right? He just needed the right horses to go along with him."

Part 2: Let's talk about Michael Jordan and his coaches.

Michael Jordan has had a few coaches during his career. When he first entered the NBA he had the head coach of Kevin Loughery. Despite the record of 38-44 and making the playoffs, he was fired at the end of Jordan's rookie season.

Jordan's second season, Stan Albeck was the coach. When Jordan came back from injury Albeck would tell Jordan that if he let Jordan play beyond 7 minutes he would get fired. I guess looking back now he should have let Michael play a few extra seconds and minutes because he was fired at the conclusion of the 1985/86 season regardless.

Doug Collins was the next head coach. Collins coached from 1986-1989. During that time he helped Jordan develop more. During their time together Jordan earned the All Star game MVP, Scoring leader, All Defensive First team and All NBA First Team. Jordan also won the regular season MVP and defensive player of the year in the same season in 1988 becoming the first player ever to do so. Most of his offense was centered on Michael Jordan. He also refused to incorporate the triangle offense that Krouse wanted him to try. Collins was fired at the end of the 1988/89 season. They would later reunite in Washington.

Michael Jordan needed Phil Jackson to win. Truth is Phil Jackson was an unproven coach with the Chicago Bulls when he first arrived. He needed great players and a front office's that would help bring the talent needed for the Bulls and Lakers to be championship contenders. Phil won two championships as a player with the Knicks in the 70s. As a coach Phil also wins six championships with Chicago and five more titles with the Lakers. Due to his success its often used against Jordan. However despite this history it's assumed Phil was already legendary, which is exaggerated. He was an assistant coach under Doug Collins. Jerry Krouse wanted Doug to use the triangle offense and he refused. Once Jerry Krouse let Doug Collins go, Phil implemented the triangle offense and the rest is history. But it cannot be said that Phil was this all time great coach before he was coaching Jordan and Pippen. It takes players to make coaches legendary.

Saying a coach takes away from a player as the GOAT is ridiculous. If that is the case why have coaches? Why not just have it be like school yard pickup game where there's no coach and let the players just play? A coach should not be used against a player. No matter if it's Michael Jordan or LeBron James.

So this narrative that Jordan couldn't win on his own is true, but LeBron James has not won on his own in retrospect. Both Michael Jordan and LeBron James have needed help. Neither has won on their own and neither has won without a good coach with them.

The ShowTime Lakers of the 1980's had the legendary coach Pat Riley, who helped lead the team to 4 championships. The Boston Celtics Won a championship with their head coach Bill Fitch in 1981. According to the LA Times, he resigned as coach when he got a phone call that the team owner was selling the team. He would be replaced with K.C. Jones where he would lead Boston to two more championships. Chuck Daly was the head coach of the Detroit Pistons in the late 1980's to early 1990's. He would help the Detroit Pistons reach three consecutive finals appearances winning two. He also coached the legendary 1992 USA Dream Team. These great teams are often referred to by the players, not the coaches. It's not until we talk about Michael Jordan does a coach ever get mentioned as why a player won a championship. Why don't we say the Lakers only won because of Pat Riley? Why don't we say Boston only won because of Bill Fitch and K.C. Jones? Why don't we say Detroit only won because of coach Chuck Daly? Coaches are important in coming up with strategies for the players to use on the court, but the credit is always give to the players. Except for when we talk about Michael Jordan and Phil Jackson.

Argument 02: Jordan's Playoff Record was 1-9 in the first Round

This is going solely on Jordan's first 3 years in the NBA and is a continuation of the previous argument. This argument is based on narrative looking solely on the Bulls playoff record. So in short the answer is yes Jordan and the Bulls did lose. Series were not as long, needing only 3 games to win a series in the first round. But do not let a playoff record from the player's early history dictate on if this player should be disqualified as the goat. If that is the case, you must disqualify the player losing much later in the playoffs like losing a championship, or if the player misses the playoffs. Did you know LeBron James has missed the playoffs and has lost in the championship? But with that I digress, so let's look more into the 1-9 argument.

Here is a look at Jordan's regular stats from his first three seasons.

Season	Games	MP	FG%	3p%	FT%	TRB	AST	STL	PTS
1984-85	82	38.3	.515	.173	.845	6.5	5.9	2.4	28.2
1985-86	18	25.1	.457	.162	.840	3.6	2.9	2.1	22.7
1986-87	82	40.0	.482	.182	.857	5.2	4.6	2.9	37.1

If you look at the seasons you see Jordan could hold his own against some of the best players in the world at this place in time. Pippen also didn't come into the NBA until Jordan's 4th season and even then Pippen wasn't an all star right away. Pippen developed under Doug Collins and Michael Jordan in his first couple of seasons. What's often left out by the media is the context that goes into the seasons that are without Pippen and what transpired during these early playoffs runs for Michael Jordan and the Chicago Bulls. So I will talk about these three seasons, who Jordan played with and against for this debate.

Michael Jordan as a rookie helped the team get to the playoffs with a record of 38-44. In the playoffs they would go against the Milwaukee Bucks in the first round. Milwaukee had a record of 59-23. Bulls had a season where they landed the 7th seed in the 1985 playoffs. Boston was the number 1 seed that year.

At the time Michael Jordan was the team's leading scorer with 28.2 points, 6.5 rebounds, 5.9 assists, 2.39 steals per game. [NBA.com website] In Jordan's rookie campaign he broke his own scoring record of 49 points in a single game in a win on February 12, 1985 against the Detroit Pistons. He set Franchise /club records on the Chicago Bulls by scoring 2,313 points, 837 field goals, attempted free throws 746, making 630 of those free throws. He also had 196 steals. Honors that Jordan received in his rookie campaign include Rookie of the year, East All Star, Sporting News Rookie of the Year, Schick Pivotal Player of the year and Seagram's NBA Player of the Year. Jordan and the Bulls lost in 4 to the Milwaukee Bucks in the first round of the playoffs (3-1).

The Bulls only all star in 84/85 season was their rookie Michael Jordan, whereas the Milwaukee Bucks had 2 all stars with Sidney Moncrief and Terry Cummings. Again proving the point that more than 1 player is needed to win.

The following season in Jordan's sophomore year in the league, he broke his foot in the 8th game of the season. Prior to that Jordan had gone 89 games where he had scored 10 or more points per game. In the 8th game of his second season he scored 8 points before injuring his foot which took him out of the game. He was out for most of the season where he missed a total of 64 games. That made it so 78% of that season Jordan missed. The poor record of the Bulls ended with 30-52 with the Bulls clinching the 8th seed in a win over Washington 105-103. The game winner was made by John Paxson who helped keep the Bulls in the playoffs for a second straight year.

The poor record is often attributed to Jordan despite him missing 78% of the games that year. In the 18 games he did play; He led his team in scoring with 22.7 points per game, 3.6 Rebounds, 2.9 Assists, 2.1 steals and 1.2 blocks per game. Due to the small number of games he played no awards were given out to him.

Due to Jordan being the best player on the team, the team record goes against him just like how poor records and missing the playoffs go against LeBron. It is not LeBron or Jordan's fault when their respective teams lose and they are not playing, however it's always tied to them by the media and fans.

The Bulls lost to the NBA champions for that 85/86 season the Boston Celtics. Chicago was the 8th seed and Boston was the number 1 seed. Boston held the best record with 67-15. They had an impressive playoff run with a playoff record of 15-3. Larry Bird was the regular season and finals MVP that year. The only All Star on Chicago that season was Michael Jordan. He did not play in the All Star game due to the injury he had, no replacement was made for the game to fill his spot.

In comparison: Boston, they had 4 all stars playing with Larry Bird, Robert Parish, Bill Walton and Kevin McHale. Even Larry Bird has said that this team he was on was the best team he's ever been on. "We had Parish, McHale and Walton. All of them are about seven foot tall that could score, run, defend. We had Danny Ainge and Dennis Johnson, and I was the small forward. So, we had a big team, and, uh, we were deep, we were big, and of all the teams I've been on, there no question, that was the best team" The Last Dance Episode 2.

Again, Chicago only all star was Michael Jordan. Jordan's teammates at the time were Quintin Dailey, Orlando Woolridge, Sidney Green and Gene Banks. None were all stars. Dailey would average that year 16.3 points. 1.9 rebounds and 1.9 assists per game. Woolridge would average 20.7 points, 5 rebounds and 3 assists. Banks would have 10.9 points, 4.4 rebounds and 3.1 assists. These were the stats that his teammates contributed during the regular season according to basketballreference.com.

Boston defeated the Chicago Bulls 3-0. However Jordan held his own against the Boston Celtics and their dynasty. Game 1: he had 49 points and was player of the game despite the loss. Game 2 Jordan goes off and scores 63 points and loses to Boston in double overtime. Larry Bird then goes on to say the famous quote "I think he's God disguised as Michael Jordan."

In game 3 it's said Jordan didn't have much left, he tired himself out. In today's game we praise players for getting triple doubles. In game 3 Jordan scored 19 points, had 10 rebounds and was 1 assist shy of a triple double. He finished the game with 9 assists. Today he would get analysts saying that's impressive for a second year player, but instead we don't. We hear he got swept by the Boston Celtics. Boston finishes the series 3-0 with a 122-104 win.

In Michael Jordan's third season the bulls were much closer to the .500 mark. Their record was 40-42, which put them at about 48.7 win percentage for the season, or 49 percent if you round up.

That year Michael Jordan was again Chicago's only All Star. He also received that seasons scoring title and was on the All NBA First Team. He played all 82 games. The team finished 5th in the central division but ended up being the 8th seed in the eastern conference playoffs. They would face the number 1 seed Boston Celtics for the second time in back to back seasons.

Chicago during that season had traded away Dailey, Woolridge and Green, giving Jordan no other scorer. That season the Bulls other top players were Charles Oakley and John Paxson. Oakley averaged 14.5 points. 13.1 rebounds, and 3.6 assists. John Paxson averaged 11.3 points, 1.7 rebounds and 5.7 assists. Jordan led the team with 37.1 points. 5.2 rebounds and 4.6 assists. Gene Banks was still on the team but he dropped a little in his stats compared to the previous season. He had 9.7 points, 4.9 rebounds and 2.7 assists per game. None of Jordan's teammates were All Stars that year.

Boston still had their 4 Hall of fame players together and were still a dynasty. They would finish the regular season with a record of 59-23. They still had 3 All Stars that season with Larry Bird, Kevin McHale and Robert Parish.

This series isn't talked about much, mainly because no huge memorable moments occurred. Chicago traded away the other players that could score. There was nothing Jordan could do when he wasn't given the same fire power as the opposition. Jordan did as well as could be expected, scoring 35 points in game 1, 42 points in game 2 and 30 points in game 3. However since Boston had more stars they overcame the emerging Chicago Bulls and won the series 3-0 for the second straight year.

Again this argument of Jordan being 1-9 in the playoffs is often looked at with no context. It's something used in the GOAT debate to just say LeBron never lost in the first round unlike Jordan. But a counter is Jordan never lost the finals unlike LeBron. So is it better to lose a few times in the first round then never lose a championship later? Or is it better to never lose in the first round and get the most championship loses in modern NBA history?

LeBron James first three seasons. Part 2 of Jordan 1-9 argument

To rebuttal the 1-9 argument I decided to create this argument of LeBron's first three seasons. This is often left out of the media outlets.

Now let's compare LeBron James first three seasons to Jordan's first three seasons. LeBron didn't face dynasties at the start of his career like Jordan did. While everyone in the media is now attacking Jordan's Bulls from those first 3 years they forget that with the 2003 Cleveland Cavaliers, they got the #1 draft pick with LeBron James. They also had no dynasts that were active at that point in time that would prevent LeBron James from making the playoffs.

Michael Jordan came into the NBA with a strong Los Angeles Lakers dynasty in the Western Conference. A strong Boston Celtics dynasty in the Eastern Conference. Then in the late 80s there was the Detroit Pistons who were a potential dynasty with going to three straight championships and winning 2 of those championships in 1989 and 1990. Pistons did not get the dynasty rank because ultimately they would lose to the ultimate Dynasty that overcame them, The Chicago Bulls. The end of Jordan's career the Los Angeles Lakers were again a dynasty with Phil Jackson leading the team as the head coach. Phil would have the best duo with Shaquille O'Neal and Kobe Bryant, both of which I listed as potential GOATS. That dynasty ended in 2004 when the Lakers lost the championship and the team disbanded. So when LeBron James was drafted no major dynasty was around for him to contend with in the Eastern Conference.

The Cleveland Cavaliers in the 2003/04 season had a record of 35-47 but missed the playoffs. LeBron James got Rookie of the Year, All Rookie first team and was the team's only All Star. In GOAT debates, you never hear analysts bringing up his rookie season unless to say Rookie of the Year or comparing teams record for their first few seasons. They don't want to say is LeBron did not make the playoffs in his first season. Why? Because Michael Jordan made the playoffs his first season despite him losing to the Bucks.

LeBron James sophomore season the Cleveland Cavaliers improved to a regular season record of 40-42. They again missed the playoffs with LeBron still being the teams only All Star. He gets All NBA second team in his sophomore season. This is left out of the GOAT debates as well. Why? In LeBron's second season he failed to make the playoffs yet again, while Jordan made the playoffs and lost to the dynasty team of the Boston Celtics. LeBron not making the playoffs is worst than getting beat in the first round. So the first 2 years of their respective careers shows Jordan making the playoffs despite a serious injury then losing in the first round. As LeBron gets no appearances in the playoffs in that same time span and no injuries.

The third season favors LeBron. LeBron not only makes it to the playoffs but he makes it to the Eastern Conference Semi Finals where he loses in 3 -4 to the Detroit Pistons. While I just spoke on how Jordan lost for a second time to Boston in 3, LeBron didn't have that same fate. Instead as a young star on the rise he did what Jordan couldn't... get to a Semi finals by his third year. While missing the playoffs the first 2 seasons he made up for it in his 3rd.

That season LeBron was again an All Star, with no other all stars on his team. He got All NBA First Team and was the All Star game MVP.

The 1-9 argument is again an attack without context. To say it should be held against Jordan for losing in the first round to the Boston Celtics is insane. The excuse given to LeBron is he loses in the finals because he didn't have the help he needed. Well this is exactly the same thing for Jordan with the exception that he faced these teams earlier, he didn't have to wait for the finals. Jordan wins this section of the argument. It's better to make the playoffs and lose in the first round than to not make the playoffs.

Argument 03: How is losing before the finals better than losing in the championship?

This one is a bit tricky to answer but it goes like this. What we remember in history are the winners. We don't talk much about the losers. We don't give out participation trophies. Can you name a sport where participation trophies are given? I can't. That's because kids are given the participation trophies to help booster their self esteem. It's not that way in professional sports.

In the work place, we are not given participation trophies, what we get are pat on the back and no write ups. We don't get trophies in real life. Maybe if you're lucky you might get employee of the month but that will be about it.

In sports it's about winning. It's about winning the championship. We don't praise the losers. And the biggest loser is always been the team that loses the championship. Why? Because most will never get another shot at that championship ring or trophy. Losing a championship is the hardest thing on an athlete. Look at some of the all time greats to have never won a championship. You can see it in their eyes how badly they wanted it. Some even move to other teams hoping the new team can help them capture that elusive championship title.

Even when we talk about the all time greats we say Magic Johnson is a five time champ, Kobe Bryant is a five time champion, Bill Russell is a 11 time champion. We don't really say much about losses. Losses do not matter when it comes to legacy talks. The only time a loss matters is when we start discussing the GOAT argument. Like I said, winning matters.

I hear some people use the Buffalo Bills as examples, On YouTube DangerProductions made a LeBron James vs Michael Jordan comparison video titled "Jordan Vs LeBron The Best GOAT Comparison." They went to 4 straight Super bowls, and lost all 4 from 1991 to 1994. They lost to the New York Giants, Washington Redskins, and Dallas Cowboys. They played the Cowboys twice. You don't hear fans saying how proud they are of the Bills for that. They don't get handed any great all time team status, or even talked about in dynasty debates, or all time great team debates because they lost. It was hard on the fans and it's hard on the team and players. The NFL and the NBA are both about winning the championship.

I recently saw sports analysts Nick Wright say Jimmy Butler's legacy is hurt by the finals loss. He tries to sell that all players' legacies are damaged when they lose a championship. So I have to say this, it does not hurt Jimmy Butler's legacy because, as of now, he's not in any GOAT conversations. Finals losses matter when we are claiming a player is the GOAT. So unless Nick is trying to say the Jimmy Butler is the GOAT, then he shouldn't be trying to confuse the masses that losing a championship hurts legacies.

Losing a finals in a players career is not something that hurts their legacy. We don't really say this players' legacy is hurt by losing the championship. Players like Charles Barkley, Patrick Ewing, and Karl Malone will always be considered great players; they just fell short of the sports ultimate prize, the championship trophy. When does finals loss matter? It matters the moment we want to claim a player as the greatest of all time. At that point a loss does matter. Legacies are about what a player did during the course of their career. GOAT's talk is about the overall accomplishments and statistics, how that player compares to everyone else that makes that player the greatest to ever play the sport. Some sports analysts don't always understand that Legacy and GOAT debates are separate.

Let's compare finals records

Player	Finals Record	Player	Finals Record
Bill Russell	11-1	LeBron James	4-6
Wilt Chamberlain	2-4	Kobe Bryant	5-2
Magic Johnson	5-4	Tim Duncan	5-1
Larry Bird	3-2	Dennis Rodman	5-1
Shaquille O'Neal	4-2	Michael Jordan	6-0

Not making it to the championship isn't necessarily better, but it allows teams to regroup sooner and come up with new strategies. They are able to look at the field and see what additions they can make in the course of the off season. What happens for the all time greats is it doesn't hurt their championship record. Championship records are like heavy weight title fights. You get up to 7 rounds unless there's a knock out. Then if you make your opponent hit the floor 4 times (each game that the opponent loses) and it's a knockout. The team wins that championship. So every player wants to make the championship, but they want to be as near perfect in the championship as they can be. Do you see what most all time greats have in common? They all have 1 loss or more with the exception of one player. Michael Jordan is the only one to have no losses in the championship. So in boxing terms he would be the undisputed undefeated heavyweight champion of the world.

Argument 04: it's about rings and finals MVP

I hear all the time *if it's about who has more rings that means Jordan isn't the GOAT. Bill Russell is.* That is absolutely true. Base on the number of championship rings Bill Russell is un-matched, and that includes all sports. No other player in any sport has won like Bill Russell has. By championships won, Bill stands alone. Didn't I tell you how some arguments goes against both LeBron and Jordan? This is one of those. So as of now, add LeBron and Jordan's rings together they have 10 championship rings between the two, Bill Russell has them both beat with 11.

Let's look at Finals MVPs now as the other part of this argument.

Bill Russell: 0

Wilt Chamberlain: 1

Magic Johnson: 3

Larry Bird:2

Kobe Bryant: 2

Shaquille O'Neal: 3

LeBron James: 4

Kareem Abdul-Jabbar: 2

Michael Jordan: 6

The only player in this list to have the most finals MVP's is Michael Jordan at 6. The rest have 4 or less currently. Michael Jordan is also the only player to win every championship and received finals MVP in each championship.

Argument 05: Michael Jordan didn't face Dynasties like LeBron James

This argument is one that I see pushed by Shannon Sharpe and Nick Wright. They claim that only LeBron James has faced dynasties and Michael Jordan didn't face any real competition.

This argument is partially true. This is also tied in with the first two arguments of Jordan 1-9 and needing Pippen. I stated earlier that there were very strong teams early in Michael Jordan's career. The 80s Lakers and 80s Celtics both had 3 or more players that were All Stars and would also be in the basketball Hall Of Fame (HOF). The Detroit Pistons were also a great team that had their own set of All Stars and HOF players. So at the very start of Jordan's career he did face opposition and did lose, with no other stars to help him.

When Jordan faced the Pistons he went up against a team with 4 hall of fame players with isiah Thomas, Joe Dumars, Dennis Rodman and Adrian Dantley. John Salley was also on that team. Salley made NBA history by being a 4 time champion on three separate teams. Did you know He won with the Bulls in the 90s? In 1990 all star game Pistons had Thomas, Dumars and Rodman. Bulls had Pippen and Jordan. Pippen would not make the all star team in 1991.

The reason the Chicago Bulls and Michael Jordan didn't face a dynasty in the 90s is because the Chicago Bulls were the dynasty. The Bulls being led by Michael Jordan were the team to beat. In 1990 Eastern Conference finals the Detroit Pistons beat the Chicago Bulls in game 7 and they did it convincingly. This led to the Bulls players to become more motivated and they got together the next day after losing to start weight training and preparing for the next season. The Bulls would go on to win 6 championships in 8 years. It's speculated that maybe had Jordan not left the game... maybe the Bulls could have won more championships. I like the narrative they would have won 8 straight or even 9 or 10 in a row, however that narrative is thrown out because no room for hypothetical's. During this span MJ would lead his team in scoring and receive multiple MVP awards.

In 1995/96 season the Chicago Bulls set a regular season record with 72-10, capping off the season with a championship. The Bulls are the only team to have 70+wins and a championship. The Bulls would also have a lot more ball movement compared to previous championship runs. This style of play was adapted after Jordan retired before the start of the 1993/94 season.

On ESPN First Take Max Kellerman stated "On his way to win 72 win games, after that to win the championship, the all time record at the time in the regular season. He swept a 60 win Shaq and Penny team in their primes, swept them! Goodbye. Then beat a 64 win team with Gary Payton and Shawn Kempt in the finals. These were 60 plus win teams. He beat the Stockton and Malone teams twice. He beat the Magic Johnson and James Worthy team when he first won his first title. This idea when he went against soft competition, the reason it seemed that way is a lot of those cats didn't win championships because Jordan beat them. They played in the Jordan era."

Max Kellerman on ESPN has pointed out how the Chicago Bulls in this season defeated two teams that got 60 wins or more. The Bulls would go on to face the Seattle Supersonics that had a regular season record of 64-18. Uneducated fans and some media members try to make it out like the Supersonics were a trash team that got over 60 wins. That's ridiculous. Gary Paton was their point guard who averaged 19.3 points, 4.2 rebounds, 7.5 assists. Shooting guard Hersey Hawkins had 15.6 points, 3.6 rebounds, 2.7 assists. Power forward Shawn Kemp had 19.6 points/11.4 rebounds, an 2.2 assists. Small Forward Detlef Schrempf had 17.1 points, 5.2 rebounds, and 4.4 assists. Ervin

Johnson their center had 5.5 points, 5.3 rebounds, and 0.6 assists. Gary Paton would go on to become a HOF inductee in 2013. He became a NBA champion after Jordan retired when he played in Miami in 2006. Two All stars in 1996 for the Supersonics were Gary Paton and Shawn Kemp.

Seattle Supersonics stats from 1996 playoffs

Player	Games	MP	FG%	3p%	FT%	TRB	AST	STL	PTS
Shawn Kemp	6	242	.551	.000	.857	10.0	2.2	1.3	23.3
Gary Payton	6	274	.444	.333	.731	6..3	7.0	1.5	18.0
Detlef Schremof	6	238	.443	.389	.875	5.0	2.5	0.5	16.3
Hersey Hawkins	6	230	.445	.273	.923	3.5	1.0	1.2	13.3
Sam Perkins	6	190	.377	.235	.810	4.7	2.0	0.5	11.2
David Wingate	6	48	.500	.500	1.000	0.3	0.0	0.0	2.5
Nate McMillian	4	51	.429	.600	1.000	2.8	1.5	0.5	2.8
Vincent Askew	4	62	.222	.200	1.000	2.5	0.5	0.5	1.8
Frank Brickowski	6	68	.222	.200	N/A	2.0	0.5	0.2	0.8
Ervin Johnson	3	20	.333	N/A	N/A	2.3	0.3	0.3	1.3
Steve Scheffler	4	8	.000	N/A	N/A	0.5	0.0	0.0	0.0
Eric Snow	6	9	.000	N/A	N/A	0.3	0.2	0.0	0.0

Chicago Bulls stats from 1996 playoffs

Player	Games	MP	FG%	3p%	FT%	TRB	AST	STL	PTS
Michael Jordan	6	252	.415	.316	.836	5.3	4.2	1.7	27.3

Scottie Pippen	6	248	.343	.231	.708	8.2	5.3	2.3	15.7
Toni Kukoc	6	177	.423	.313	.800	4.8	3.5	0.8	13.0
Luc Longley	6	170	.574	N/A	.727	3.8	2.2	0.5	11.7
Dennis Rodman	6	225	.486	N/A	.579	14.7	2.5	0.8	7.5
Ron Harper	6	116	.375	.308	.917	2.2	1.7	0.7	6.5
Steve Kerr	6	113	.303	.182	.857	0.8	0.8	0.2	5.0
Randy Brown	6	49	.500	.500	.500	0.3	0.8	0.7	2.8
Bill Wennington	6	42	.667	N/A	.500	0.5	0.2	0	2.8
Jud Buechlet	6	33	.222	0.0	0.0	0.0	0.2	0.7	0.7
John Salley	5	15	.000	N/A	N/A	0.2	0.4	0.0	0.0

This was an competitive series. However, players on the Chicago Bulls like Dennis Rodman were on their A games. Dennis Rodman that season had acquired the rebounding title, making him one of the most dangerous at giving his teams more opportunities to get second chances at scoring. This continued into the 1996 finals where in game 6 he tied the NBA Finals record of 11 offensive rebounds, a record he shares with Elvin Hayes. Michael Jordan that same season set a record of winning his 8th Scoring title passing Wilt Chamberlain who has seven. Jordan of course would go on to win two more scoring titles over the next few seasons. Toni Kukoc would go on to win the 6th man of the year award. This Bulls team is said to be the greatest team in the history of the sport. While the 2016 Golden State Warriors did break the regular season record, the team failed to deliver a championship in this record setting season. The Chicago Bulls in 1996 had a 72-10 record and they won the championship in six games.

The truth is Jordan was a part of this dynasty and no great Hall of fame player could beat him once he had his dynasty together. Hall of Fame players Jordan beat by them being "Knocked out of the playoffs includes Charles Barkley, Vlade Divac, Clyde Drexler, Joe Dumars, Patrick Ewing, Magic Johnson, Karl Malone, Reggie Miller, Alonzo Mourning, Chris Mullin, Dikembe Mutombo, Shaquille O'Neal, Robert Parish, Gary Paton, Dennis Rodman, Jack Sikma, John Stockton, Isiah Thomas, Dominique Wilkins, and James Worthy." Chris Rosvoglou of thespun.com *The 20 Hall of famers Michael Jordan Knocked Out of the Playoffs*.

LeBron James supporters say LeBron only lost because he faced Dynasties. The truth is LeBron ran into the same thing that Jordan faced. He ran into a team that was more established and had more stars. Lebron went to the finals where the inexperienced Cavaliers were out gunned and outmatched. 2007 San Antonio Spurs had Tim Duncan a future HOF player. Tony Parker who would win Finals MVP in that series. Manu Ginobili who would win 4 championships in his career, and Robert Horry would win seven championships with a record of 7-0 (sometimes used to say he is better than Jordan because he won more rings). Then there is a cast of role players. Simply put the Spurs would go on to win the series in a sweep, 4 games to none.

LeBron would face the spurs two more times in the finals. 2013 and 2014. The Heat would win in 2013 and would come from a legacy saving 3 point shot made by Ray Allen. The Spurs would come back the following season and defeat the Heat. It's said LeBron lost to the Spurs because they are a dynasty, but truth be told they are going off of Tim Duncan being 5-1 in the NBA finals, which is spread over 20 years. The Spurs were not a dynasty, just a really good team. Miami was just as good with James, Wade, Bosh and Allen. There was only one team that LeBron faced that is a dynasty and that's the Golden State Warriors. LeBron had potential to have dynasties for teams he played for. Had his team won more with either the Miami Heat or Cleveland Cavaliers, either team could have become a dynasty with LeBron leading the way.

The Golden State Warriors drafted and developed the majority of their roster for their championship runs. This made them become the latest Dynasty in the NBA. Their style of play being very similar to the rapid ball movement that was used by the Chicago Bulls in the mid to late 90's. Their head coach Steve Kurr who played for the Bulls and was coached by Phil Jackson and played with Michael Jordan. The Warriors would win the 2015 championship against LeBron led Cavaliers. Golden State would have a roster that included Stephen Curry, Klay Tompsons, Draymond Green and Andre Iguodala. Many say they only won because Kyrie Irving and Kevin Love were hurt. But even with that said the Warriors in 2015 were not a proven team and it was not known if the Cavs were a locked team to win. The fact that the Warriors won the championship made the Cavs and LeBron fans say *Asterisks*.

In 2016 the Golden State Warriors broke the 1996 Chicago Bulls single season wins record with 73-9. They would go on to lose the championship in seven games to the Cavaliers. This however is not without controversy. LeBron James gets Draymond Green suspended, mainly from him complaining about being kicked in game 4. Draymond kicking LeBron in the groin area led to him being suspended. While this should not be a big deal it did shift momentum to the Cavs. In the closing minutes of game 7 the Warriors go nearly four and a half minutes where they do not score. This was unheard of when this Warriors team is supposed to be one of the most high powered offensive teams in the modern era.

LeBron also blocked a layup from Andre Iguodala and this block is hailed by many as his most impressive finals/playoff defensive stances made by LeBron. This again leads to controversy by many believing it was goal tending by LeBron. I have looked at this block several times and honestly it does appear to be a missed goal tending call. The Cavaliers would win the 2016 championship, beating the 73-9 win regular season Warriors.

What made the championship more special is the Cavs did it by being the first team ever to come back 3-1 deficit in the finals to win. The Warriors came back from a 3-1 deficit in their previous series against the Oklahoma City Thunder. The Warriors after 2016 go get Kevin Durant. I mentioned Kevin Durant as an honorable mention for future GOAT debates, especially if he wins more championships. The Warriors would win 3 championships in 5 straight finals appearances. This dominance helped the Warriors become a dynasty. The Warriors would be 3-1 against LeBron during this championship reign.

Due to these I often see LeBron fanatics saying these finals loses should not be held against him, he was out manned. Yet this exact same scenario occurred to Jordan in the 1-9 argument. Jordan was simply out manned. The truth is this narrative of only LeBron facing great teams will persist. I just explained how Jordan faced the Celtics and Pistons where both teams had 4 hall of fame players and Jordan was the only competition. Basketball is a team sport, so no great player has won on his own. In comparison to LeBron, GSW had 4 all stars with Iguodala, Green, Curry and Thompson. The Warriors trade away Iguodala and get Kevin Durant.

In factuality LeBron being the only one to face these dynasties or great teams and Jordan facing plumbers and garbage men is false. It's an attempt to discredit Jordan's championship runs or any great team in the 80s. I even saw a video on YouTube of some ill advised and non educational LeBron fan say the 80's Boston Celtics team had Larry Bird who was a Plummer, another player he referred to as a off duty security guard, and then a different Celtic as a garbage man. If I recall right, around this time Celtics have legends and are champions and champion contenders. The fact the guy calls Larry a plumber show's he has no knowledge of what he is talking about. I have never heard any sports talk show refer to these players like that. This is part of the reason fans of LeBron are very disrespectful to not just Michael Jordan, but also to Larry Bird. Jordan beat legends and all time great players. But it sounds better to say he faced no competition for fans advocating for LeBron James.

Argument 06: Is 4-6 greater than 6-0?

First presented by fans online right after the Lakers won the 2020 championship, mainly in online live chat streams on YouTube. This has since been included on shows First Things First and Undisputed by Shannon Sharpe and Nick Wright saying that regardless of LeBron's record, he is the GOAT because he has been to the finals on ten separate occasions.

This argument is going by LeBron getting to the finals 10 separate times, regardless of the outcome of his record. Like I said before, winning matters. We don't give participation trophies in the NBA. So this narrative is flat out wrong. Never losing the finals is better than making the finals 10 times and losing 6 of those championships. Don't get me wrong, It's impressive LeBron made it to the finals this many times in his career, but he has underachieved for him being considered the greatest player of all time in some people's eyes. If he's the G.O.A.T. shouldn't he win more often if he's the greatest player ever? Never losing the championship is more impressive and has rarely been achieved by most players. It's also rare in most sports to have a perfect championship record. Never losing a championship is almost impossible. Only a few NBA players can say they never lost a championship, but only one of those players can claim he was the best player to never lose, Michael Jordan.

Argument 07: Has any player won finals MVP in every championship the player was in?

While this question is never really on the networks, the topic of championships and Finals MVP's are brought up during the debates. Skip Bayless is one that uses this during his arguments on Undisputed. "All I know is [Michael] Jordan is six and 0 in the finals with six finals MVP's."

The answer to this question is yes. Only 1 player in NBA history who has won every championship he was in and got finals MVP in each championship. That player is Michael Jordan.

LeBron James has won 4 finals MVP's in all four championships he won but he has not won finals MVP in every finals appearance. Rob Parker from Fox Sports has pointed out "LeBron has the most finals loses of any former MVP." Due to him not just losing the finals but not getting finals MVP in every appearance is a negative for him.

Argument 08: Scoring means the player is the G.O.A.T.

Mainly I see Shannon Sharpe on Undisputed push for the scoring argument because as of today it is projected for LeBron James to pass Kareem Abdul-Jabbar on the all time scoring list in the next few seasons. So as a way to help promote the Longevity argument, this scoring argument is implemented.

Since we are talking about scoring, I decided to take it further and break it down.

Currently in the NBA there are three parts to this argument.

One: is who has the most points scored in a single game? That is Wilt Chamberlain who scored 100 points in a game and that record has stood the test of time and remains to this day. Wilt is the GOAT for scoring the most points in a single game.

Two: Who has averaged the most points in winning a championship? That would go to Michael Jordan. By year these were his points per game for each championship.

1991: 31.2

1992: 35.8

1993: 41

1996: 27.3

1997: 32.3

1998: 33.5

Michael was a scorer and it showed in each championship, helping him earn Finals MVP in all 6 finals appearances. Michael Jordan is the GOAT for scoring the most points while winning a championship and getting finals MVP.

Three: player that holds the all time scoring leader record is Kareem Abdul-Jabbar. His record has stood for since his retirement in 1989. He has 38,387 career points. So at this current place in time Kareem Abdul-Jabbar is the GOAT as far as career points. LeBron does aim to challenge this and will take approximately two more seasons to surpass Kareem as the NBA's all time leading scorer.

Argument 09: G.O.A.T's create Dynasties

I will have to give Chris Broussard from the Fox radio show the Odd Couple as making this original argument. He has pointed out when going on TV shows The Herd, Undisputed and First Things First about how LeBron has not been part of any dynasty, and Michael Jordan created a dynasty in Chicago.

Here are my inputs.

Magic Johnson was drafted in 1979 and he was playing along side great players like Kareem Abdul Jabbar, Jamaal Wilkes, Norm Nixon and Jim Chones. Magic Johnson in his rookie year wins the championship and finals MVP. He came into the league as a winner. He however did not have to make the Lakers into a dynasty. As far as winning a championship his rookie season Magic is the GOAT. He is not the GOAT in creating a dynasty because the Lakers were already a dynasty being led by Kareem.

LeBron James has gone to the championship 10 times, this has been mentioned a few times now. But he has not created a dynasty at any team he's played on. He has not been on a team that dominated and won for several years. He by himself went to 8 straight finals on two separate teams the Miami Heat and Cleveland Cavaliers. During those eight years he only won 3 championships in that span.

Michael Jordan helped the Chicago Bulls go from a bunch of losers to a dynasty. The Bulls dominated the majority of the 90s, winning 6 championships in 8 years. During this time Bulls had the formula they needed to stay relevant. During Jordan's reign the 1996 Chicago Bulls set a record 72-10 and sealed the deal with a championship. The 2016 Golden State Warriors were not able to get a championship despite them getting a 73-9 record to beat the Bulls. Depending who you talk to these two teams are argued as the greatest teams ever in the NBA.

Bleacher Report did a ranking a few years ago on all time greatest teams. #2: 1996 Chicago Bulls. #1: 2016 Golden State Warriors. This was based just on regular season wins.

Kobe Bryant and Shaq had a dynasty going from 2000 to 2004 winning a three-peat from 2000 to 2002. This Lakers dynasty was not as long as Magic and Kareem's Lakers from the 70s and 80s.

Argument 10: Who has the most unstoppable shot?

I don't see this topic really brought up in the GOAT debates. Probably because unless they are talking about Kareem Abdul-Jabbar, there is not talk about un-block-able shots. On ESPN *Get Up* talk about shot's that are un-guardable in the NBA. Jalon Rose talked about different players that are in the NBA and players from the past. He mentions how different players were able to create a shot that was unique to that player.

From the players I have mentioned as potential GOAT's I looked at players that had an iconic shot or are known for their shot.

LeBron James loves to drive to the rim and either dunk or put up a layup. His shooting percentage is higher than the other greats due to this being 50% from the field. But that's expected when most of his shots are within 3 feet and less. Mainly with layups and dunks he would be right at the rim. Yet none of his dunks or layups are dominant or un-guardable. Instead he has made an arsenal of different shots that he can use at any moment, making him one of the most efficient scorers in today's game. He has developed his own turnaround jump shot which because of how high he jumps makes defending it extremely difficult.

Kareem Abdul-Jabbar started doing a shot called the sky hook because for a period of time dunks were not allowed. Thus he developed a shot that even today remains un-guardable. During his impressive career he not only ranked up his career points but he also could score at will.

Michael Jordan is said to be a pure shooter, a scorer, an assassin. He went out onto the floor to annihilate his opponents. As he got older he had to develop more ways to score, so he added the fade away jump shot that appeared could not be blocked. While this was a deadly shot to his opponents it's not the most dominant or unstoppable shot.

Kobe Bryant is a gifted scorer, but many look at him as a carbon copy to Jordan. Like his turn around fade away shot. Still was an impressive shot, even if it mimicked Jordan.

The most unstoppable shot goes to Kareem as the GOAT for this argument.

Argument 11: Who's the best passer of all time?

I see Shannon Sharpe use the argument of rebounds and assists makes LeBron the GOAT, that because LeBron James has more it so it means he's better. During the course of LeBron James career he's been able to get over 8,000 assists. He is praised for his passing abilities and every sports show will show him *dishing* a pass to an open teammate. The argument for his passing is based on his assists. Yet many former players and other sports talk show hosts like Chris Broussard don't put LeBron James as the greatest passer. So who is the best passer of all time?

I'll give you a hint, it's not Michael Jordan or LeBron James.

Magic Johnson is considered the greatest passer in NBA history, averaging 11.2 assists per game he had innovated the way we look at basketball with long range bounce passes and no look passes getting his teammates in position to win the game. But right next to him is Larry Bird. My opinion is that Larry is the best passer of all time but due to more dominance by Magic and the Lakers, I have to give it to Magic Johnson.

Argument 12: Who's the best rebounder of all time

I don't really see this used in the GOAT debates, but because it is a stat that is still used for the players, I am still incorporating it into my debates.

You will see in the Last Dance Documentary, former players and even sports analysts. That Dennis Rodman is the greatest rebounder ever in the history of the sport. He had it down to a science, and would practice how the different type of shots would determine where the ball would come down. He was able to study so many players that he perfected this aspect of the game. Dennis Rodman averaged 13.1 rebounds per game, scoring 7.3 points per game, and 1.8 assists per game.

While I love Dennis Rodman, and I do have him as one of the best rebounders and defenders of all time, he's not my greatest rebounder of all time. For this, I looked more at two of my potential GOATs, Bill Russell and Wilt Chamberlain.

This one was a close one, between Bill Russell and Wilt Chamberlain. Bill was an astonishing blocker and an amazing rebounder. He averaged 22.5 rebounds per game and the fact of him winning 11 championships really weighs in for this conversation.

Wilt Chamberlain averaged just a bit more with 22.9 rebounds per game. Yet his team didn't win as much as Bill Russell's Celtics.

Despite Wilt averaging slightly more I have to go with Bill Russell because like I said winning matters. GOAT argument for Rebounding goes to Bill Russell.

Argument 13: Greatest defensive stops and scoring ever in NBA history

I don't really see this category in the debates either, so I created it to show how the last minute or two of the game can impact not just the teams but the player's legacies. So for the player to have the most iconic moment these are what I was looking for:

Does the player have an offensive moment to help them win the game?

Does that same player make a defensive stance to win the same ballgame immediately before or after the offensive moment?

The order in which those two questions are can be flipped but essentially I was looking for their moments that helped my GOAT candidates on winning a championship with these two questions.

#3: LeBron James: in 2016 LeBron got the block that helped him achieve the one and only championship the Cleveland Cavaliers ever got. In the final minutes he was able to chase down Andre Iguodala and block the shot from behind and hit the ball off the backboard with 1:09 left in the game. This would result in J. R. Smith recovering the ball. This would then lead to Kyrie Irving shooting a 3 pointer to give the Cavaliers their first ever championship.

#2: Bill Russell: in 1957 Bill would be in the championship game. The series is against the Hawks and the series went seven games. In the final minute of the game Bill scores a layup to put Boston up by one. Right after that the Hawks pass from one end of the floor to the other to put the ball in the hands of Jack Coleman. As he went for a shot Bill Russell jumps and blocks the ball off the backboard. The Celtics get the ball back and win their first ever championship [Bill Russell Documentary].

#1: Michael Jordan: in the 1998 NBA finals Michael Jordan has the most Iconic moment in sports history. In the final minute John Stockton scores a three pointer to put the Utah Jazz up by three. Jordan right after that in just four seconds he scores a layup to bring the Bulls to pull within 1 point. With the Jazz up by one Karl Malone gets the ball and instead of Jordan following after Hornasect he stays by the basket and steals the ball away from Karl Malone with 19 seconds left in the game. Jordan sees Phil isn't calling time out so he takes the ball down the court. He pushes off of Brian Russell and makes a jump shot with 5.2 seconds left. Jordan put the Bulls up by 1, with the score of 87-86. These three plays all went off of Jordan scoring twice and getting one of the most iconic defensive stops in NBA finals history. The result of these three plays happening simultaneously, led to the Chicago Bulls winning a sixth title and a second three-peat.

Argument 14: LeBron has no help and he takes his teams to the championships

This argument is mainly a myth I see Nick Wright push, he likes to make fans believe LeBron James never has help and he gets all of his teams to the championship with no help.

To debunk this myth, I listed a brief history of his championship runs.

Cleveland first time around: no clear all star to help LeBron, they lose a championship in 2007 [to the San Antonio Spurs] and LeBron leaves by 2010. This is probably the only time the statement is true, LeBron took his team to a championship with no all star next to him for help.

In 2011 he leaves Cleveland to join his friends with the Miami Heat. LeBron has 2 all stars with Dwayne Wade and Chris Bosh in his first 2 seasons with the Heat. In 2013 the Heat acquires Ray Allen to join the team. During his time in Miami many considered him starting the super team era in today's basketball. The Heat win 2 championships in 4 years and is considered underachieving with the amount of talent they had.

In 2015 LeBron returns to Cleveland. The Cleveland Cavaliers had drafted Kyrie Irving who became a two time All Star and won the All Star game MVP in 2014. They are joined by Kevin Love who was a three time all star from the Minnesota Timberwolves. Those three go on to win 1 championship in 3 years. 2018 Cleveland loses Kyrie but they still have Love. They get Isiah Thomas, Derrick Rose and Dwayne Wade. By trade deadline team changes its roster and the Cavs received players Larry Nance Jr, Jordan Clarkson, George Hill and Rodney Hood. Players such as Darrick Rose, Dwayne Wade and Isaiah Thomas are traded away. Several media outlets claim these trades really upgraded the roster. The Cavaliers make it to the finals where they are ultimately swept in 4 games, losing once again to the Golden State Warriors.

2019 LeBron heads to Los Angeles to play with the Lakers. He is joined with Boston Celtics point guard and former champion Rajon Rondo. He has a young core of players that include Brandon Ingram, Lonzo Ball, Kyle Kuzma, Josh Hart. The Lakers fail to make the playoffs, many blame the young inexperienced roster. LeBron enters his playoff mode earlier than usual but it's too late, Lakers fall further out of the playoffs losing to bad teams like the Phoenix Suns.

In 2019/20 season the team trades most of their young core for all star big man Anthony Davis. They also have former all stars and former defensive player of the year on the Lakers by adding DeMarcus Cousins and Dwight Howard. Rajon Rondo is still a great player and is considered one of the teams leaders. The Lakers with LeBron missed the playoffs in 2019 but are champions in 2020.

2020/21: As I finish writing this free agency is happening. The Lakers appear to be in a rebuild despite dominating the league and holding the western conference's best record last season. The only players to resign and appear safe are Clutch Sports clients LeBron James, Anthony Davis and Kentavious Caldwell-Pope. A majority of last seasons championship roster was traded away or wasn't resigned.

Point is no player can win by themselves. If you look at my argument it pretty much says LeBron is always needing stars to win. But that's true for every superstar out there and every team. Even with the Lakers current construct they made acquisitions in acquiring other stars besides Anthony Davis.

Players like Danny Green went against LeBron during the Heat vs Spurs championship joins The Lakers. When Danny is in LA he wins his third championship. After the Lakers win the championship both Danny green and LeBron James become 1 of 4 players in history to win championships with three separate franchises.

The narrative used in saying LeBron has no teammates that are significant is a total lie. It's aimed to try to create an argument that's one sided, but I just pointed out how LeBron has had help. Yet the narrative is he has no help? Didn't he have Wade and Bosh when he lost to an inferior team the Dallas Mavericks? These narratives are used in arguments as being presented as facts but are often more of an emotional argument. They try to hide behind enough facts to make their statements sound true rather than admit its feelings. The teammates argument is applied to both and both need teammates to win, I believe I said this before.

Argument 15: Longevity

The Longevity argument is from several people, Nick Wright, Shannon Sharpe, Kendrick Perkins and Chris Broussard. These sports analysts will talk about LeBron's longevity and how impressive his stats are because of it. These stats can be great for LeBron James career totals. It will help elevate him in the GOAT debate for those of his fans. However, I decided to show how longevity can be used against LeBron in this section.

Here's another statement that could be believed when comparing the two players, LeBron James and Michael Jordan. LeBron has dominated the NBA for 17 years versus Jordan who was dominant for 10 years.

If you are a LeBron fan would you say he's the ultimate juggernaut for staying in his prime for the past 16 to 17 years? What I hear from Nick Wright say is that no one has ever been like LeBron. That he has had the East on lockdown for 15 seasons before heading to the west to play for the Lakers. They praise him for his longevity.

As Nick Wright has said "He's bigger, he's stronger, he's faster, he's more durable." He wants to make the case that as a basketball player, he's overall better.

I saw after LeBron won his fourth ring that Nick Wright would say Jordan wasn't dominant and everyone ate off his plate. That other athletes won championships during his career. He then lists a few players that were known to have won championships mainly in the 80s, 1990, 1995, 2002 and 2003 seasons. While I was listening to this I couldn't help but wonder why his colleagues didn't stop him and say, well hasn't everyone in the modern NBA ate off LeBron's plate? There are only 2 superstars that he faced in the finals that as of today have no championship rings. Those players being James Harden and Russell Westbrook.

LeBron has played 17 seasons, even though he was injured for part of the season in 2019. I still have to include it because we count Jordan's horrid sophomore season where he missed 78% of the season. So if we count Jordan's injured season, we count LeBron's. So let's look at this Longevity argument.

Now LeBron said after winning the championship with the Lakers that "I want my damn respect too." He didn't aim this statement at me in particular, but at all of the fans and analysts everywhere. So in a way he might not like what I'm about to say.

Since the 2003-04 season, LeBron has played for 17 years in the NBA [04, 05, 06, 07, 08. 09. 10. 11. 12. 13. 14, 15, 16, 17, 18, 19, 20]. He has won 4 championships in that time span. That's 13 years where he hasn't won. In context Jordan played 15 years. So LeBron has almost as many seasons where he didn't win a championship that's near Jordan's career length. Jordan in 1998 had played 13 seasons. 11 of those seasons were full seasons. One season was shortened due to injury in 1985/86. The next shortened season was his out of retirement year where he played 18 games in 1995. In that time frame of his 13 seasons he won 6 championships. Six titles in eight years seem to show more dominance compared to 4 championships spread over 17 years.

However let's put it in this context. LeBron's first championship appearance was in 2007. So let's show from his first championship to his more current [*07*, 08, 09, 10, *11*, **12, 13**, 14, *15*, **16**, *17*, *18*, 19, **20**]. I decided to use bigger text and bold to show the years LeBron won the championship.

Italic sized means there was a loss in the championship. Regular black text means there was no finals appearance. Using this we have the finals record of 4-6. If we put this time to add non championship appearances as a loss that is a record of 4-10. So let's change it to when he Started winning his first championship to the latest championship. 2012 to 2020 [**12, 13**, *14*, *15*, **16**, *17*, *18*, 19, **20**]. If we look at this time span which is nine seasons long, he holds a record of 4-4. If the 2019 injured season is counted as a loss, then it's 4-5. But for argument sake let's keep it at 4-4.

Jordan played for 15 seasons [85, 86, 87, 88, 89, 90, **91, 92, 93**, 95, **96, 97, 98**, 02, 03]. So let's show from his first championship to his last championship [**91, 92, 93**, 95, **96, 97, 98**]. This is actually a seven year span, because I cannot include a season in which he did not play in the NBA because he was retired. In this he is 6-0 in the finals. If we include the year he didn't make the championship as a loss, then it becomes 6-1.

Lets now put every season where they did not win a championship as a loss and add it to their finals losses.

James: 4-13.

Jordan 6-9.

Of these two records who's is better? Based on their careers added into their finals records still puts Jordan as having the better record. So Longevity is great for accumulative stats, but it needs to be said that Longevity can be used against great players too. I also like to point this out, when saying because a player has more points, rebounds, assists, steals or blocks in their career, it doesn't always mean that player is better. For example Karl Malone is currently 2nd in all time career points scored, but he has never won a championship, nor has he ever been considered better than Kareem, Kobe, Jordan, LeBron or any of the other top scorers. Kobe passed Jordan and it helped his career accolades but is it has not placed him as being better than Jordan. This same thing applies to LeBron. He will break many records, but just because he has more of the stats doesn't mean he is better than the other all time greats.

In the media, we hear how longevity is so impressive because we haven't seen a player be this good for his whole career. While LeBron has been a good player, he hasn't been the best player until after he went to Miami and won his first championship. He wasn't considered the best; Kobe was considered the best by many up to 2010. While they never played each other in the championship it would have been a dream match for fans to see. Nick Wright says Kobe failed to face LeBron when LeBron started making his championship runs. But he leaves out that before LeBron started making his championship runs with the Miami Heat, LeBron had a chance for the Cleveland Caveliers to face the Los Angeles Lakers had he been able to get his team to the finals. Had LeBron made it to the championship in 2009 or 2010 he would have faced Kobe Bryant in the Championship, this is left out from TV Shows. Not many have played at a high level for most of their careers, but LeBron has taken care of himself to give him the longevity argument. He is rarely hurt and that helps his case. What do you think? Does Longevity help or hurt his case as the G.O.A.T?

Argument 16: LeBron hasn't had any good coaches

I see Nick Wright push this as well as Shannon Sharpe. Both have concluded that LeBron has not had any legendary coaches and because of this that's kind of why he has some losses. Had he had a legendary coach, he would probably have an even better record or the best all time championship record.

So I am going to look at this argument. LeBron James hasn't stayed with any coach long enough to claim that that coach would be an all time great coach. He has had a couple of coaches that he has won with.

Miami Heat's Eric Spoelstra has been to the championship 5 times in his career. Granted 4 of those times he had a super-team with LeBron, Wade and Bosh from 2011 to 2014. Then he was in the 2020 finals, where his best player is Jimmy Butler. The Heat was a 5th seed entering the playoffs inside the Orlando Bubble. The finals match in the Orlando Bubble was the first time Spoelstra made it back to the finals since 2014 and his team went against the LeBron led L.A. Lakers. Many thought the Lakers would sweep the Heat yet somehow they made the series go to six games. The Heat lost the 2020 finals but Spoelstra does deserve credit for making this a better series than was expected.

Tyronn Lue coached LeBron in Cleveland and won a championship with him in 2016. Had they stuck around together maybe they could have won more together? Together they overcame the Golden State Warriors. The Warriors would break the all time regular season wins record. They also came back from a 3 – 1 deficit to win this championship. This is something no other team, players or coaches have ever done prior. This puts Tyronn in the upper echelon of coaches even if he's not legendary yet. Point is he could he on his way. He also is over looked by winning a championship as a player with Phil Jackson as the coach of the Lakers. He also played with Michael Jordan in Washington. So Tyronn has played with great players and was coached by a legend. It is likely he learned something from Phil Jackson and Michael Jordan. This experience with those two might have helped in developing plays and strategies in overcoming the Warriors. It also helped that Tyronn Lue had the best player on the planet on his team with LeBron James.

Frank Vogel hasn't done much in his coaching career, mainly due to him being against LeBron in the Eastern Conference. Once Frank and LeBron were together not only did they take the Lakers to the number 1 seed in the Western Conference in 2020; they win a championship together in their first season together. Is Frank Vogel an all time great coach, again only time will tell?

The Lakers with Frank Vogel and LeBron James are favored to win the championship in 2021, this would put them at 2-0 together in the championship. Of course that is as of now hypothetical, so I can't give it value. However, if they continue to win together, he could very well be considered a legendary coach. Like I said back in argument 1, players are what make a coach legendary.

Argument 17: Does LeBron James make his teammates better?

With this argument I had to look at stats of his teams. Before playing with LeBron and when they played together.

Dwayne Wade

Season	Team	Games	FG%	3p%	FT%	TRB	AST	STL	PTS
2003-04	MIA	61	.465	.302	.747	247	275	86	991
2004-05	MIA	77	.478	.289	.762	397	520	121	1854
2005-06	MIA	75	.495	.171	.783	430	503	146	2040
2006-07	MIA	51	.491	.266	.807	239	384	107	1397
2007-08	MIA	51	.469	.286	.758	214	354	87	1254
2008-09	MIA	79	.491	.317	.765	398	589	173	2386
2009-10	MIA	77	.476	.300	.761	373	501	142	2045
2010-11	MIA	76	.500	.306	.758	485	346	111	1941
2011-12	MIA	49	.497	.268	.791	237	255	82	1082
2012-13	MIA	69	.521	.258	.725	344	352	128	1463
2013-14	MIA	54	.545	.281	.733	241	252	79	1028
2014-15	MIA	62	.470	.284	.768	219	299	73	1331
2015-16	MIA	74	.456	.159	.793	302	344	79	1409
2016-17	CHI	60	.434	.310	.794	270	288	86	1096
2017-18	TOT	67	.438	.288	.714	252	228	61	765
2017-18	CLE	46	.455	.329	.701	181	163	42	513
2017-18	MIA	21	.409	.220	.745	71	65	19	252
2018-19	MIA	72	.433	.330	.708	285	301	59	1083

Wade was a champion in the 2006 finals and was the finals MVP. He was an all star leading up to him being joined by LeBron James and Chris Bosh. Stats that show he was peaking getting more points rebounds and assists in the seasons when he did not play with LeBron James. He averaged 5 rebounds per game in 2008/09 and 2012/13 campaigns but he did not improve statistically when playing with LeBron James in Miami or Cleveland.

Chris Bosh

Season	Team	Games	FG%	3p%	FT%	TRB	AST	STL	PTS
2003-04	TOR	75	.459	.357	.701	7.2	1.0	0.8	11.5
2004-05	TOR	81	.471	.300	.760	8.9	1.9	0.9	16.8
2005-06	TOR	70	.505	.000	.816	9.2	2.6	0.7	22.5
2006-07	TOR	69	.496	.343	.785	10.7	2.5	0.6	22.6
2007-08	TOR	67	.494	.400	.844	8.7	2.6	0.9	22.3
2008-09	TOR	77	.487	.245	.817	10.0	2.5	0.9	22.7
2009-10	TOR	70	.518	.364	.797	10.8	2.4	0.6	24.0
2010-11	MIA	77	.496	.240	.815	8.3	1.9	0.8	18.7
2011-12	MIA	57	.487	.286	.821	7.9	1.8	0.9	18.0
2012-13	MIA	74	.535	.284	.798	6.8	1.7	0.9	16.6
2013-14	MIA	79	.516	.339	.820	6.8	1.1	1.0	16.2
2014-15	MIA	44	.460	.375	.772	7.0	2.2	0.9	21.1
2015-16	MIA	53	.467	.365	.795	7.4	2.4	0.7	19.1

When comparing the Toronto Raptors stats to the Miami Heat stats, Bosh took a decline in his numbers. If LeBron is making his teammates better, they will put up better stats. Chris Bosh took a decline in points, rebounds and assists per game while being teamed with LeBron James and Dwayne Wade. According to his statistics, Bosh was more productive in Toronto compared to Miami.

Ray Allen

Season	Team	Games	FG%	3p%	FT%	TRB	AST	STL	PTS
2007-08	BOS	73	.445	.398	.907	3.7	3.1	0.9	17.4
2008-09	BOS	79	.480	.409	.952	3.5	2.8	0.9	18.2
2009-10	BOS	80	.477	.363	.913	3.2	2.6	0.8	16.3
2010-11	BOS	80	.491	.444	.881	3.4	2.7	1.0	16.5
2011-12	BOS	46	.458	.453	.915	3.1	2.4	1.1	14.2
2012-13	MIA	79	.449	.419	.886	2.7	1.7	0.8	10.9
2013-14	MIA	73	.442	.375	.905	2.8	2.0	0.7	9.6

For Ray Allen, I did not include his entire career, because I didn't need to. The myth LeBron makes his teammates better is again debunked and in the two years Ray Allen played in Miami. The 2012-13 and 2013-14 seasons were his least productive seasons. He took a decline in his field goal percentage, his three point percentage, free throw percentage, rebounds, assists and points per game. Truth is he was brought on the team to help give them more depth. He may not have been a top 10 player, but was always considered an assassin and a sniper in the game of basketball. His abilities to shoot the ball was proven during the 2013 NBA finals when he helped save LeBron's legacy by making the iconic three pointer. He is still a player that is an All Star and HOF. He was the 4th biggest addition to the Miami Heat and remains a valid point on LeBron needing more stars to win. Many also still considered Ray Allen to be a very valuable asset when Miami acquired him.

Kyrie Irving

Season	Team	Games	FG%	3p%	FT%	TRB	AST	STL	PTS
2011-12	CLE	51	.469	.399	.872	3.7	5.4	1.1	18.5
2012-13	CLE	59	.452	.391	.855	3.7	5.9	1.5	22.5
2013-14	CLE	71	.430	.358	.861	3.6	6.1	1.5	20.8
2014-15	CLE	75	.468	.415	.863	3.2	5.2	1.5	21.7
2015-16	CLE	53	.448	.321	.885	3.0	4.7	1.1	19.6
2016-17	CLE	72	.473	.401	.905	3.2	5.8	1.2	25.2
2017-18	BOS	60	.491	.408	.889	3.8	5.1	1.1	24.4
2018-19	BOS	67	.487	.401	.873	5.0	6.9	1.5	23.8
2019-20	BRK	20	.478	.394	.922	5.2	6.4	1.4	27.4

Kyrie Irving played with LeBron in 2014/15 to 2016/17. He was showing improvement each year until LeBron returned. Kyrie Irving dropped in rebounds, assists, blocks, and steals he made per game during his three years playing with LeBron. He did manage to score more points per game and his free throw percentage went up in his last season in Cleveland in 2016-17. After the Cleveland Cavaliers lost to the Golden State Warriors in the 2016-17 NBA Finals in five games, Kyrie requested to be traded. He even demanded the trade and threatened to sit out the season by getting surgery due to him not wanting to play with LeBron James. This was covered extensively on the FS1 sports broadcast Undisputed. Shannon Sharpe and Skip Bayless would discuss about Kyrie wanting to get out of Cleveland. When Kyrie Irving went to Boston he was battling injuries and took a small decline in his production due to him not playing as much. He wanted to be the focal point of the offense and thought he could be a leader to this franchise. The first year in Boston, he got injured and watched his team have a deep playoff run without him being there. In his second year in Boston he returned and it was discovered that there were chemistry issues with him and the other Boston players. Kyrie would be saying to the media how he is thinking of resigning and will be back after that season. This was again covered extensively by Shannon Sharpe and Skip Bayless on Undisputed.

The Milwaukee Bucks would go on to beat the Boston Celtics in the Eastern Conference Semi-Finals 4-1. At the conclusion of the season Kyrie leaves the Boston Celtics for the Brooklyn Nets. While playing in Brooklyn he started to get to his old self, his stats were starting to get to an All Star level before he reinjured himself. His production over the past 4 years has had his points fluctuate from 23 points to 27 points per game. He has gradually improved with his stats but over the past few seasons has hit a wall where he seems to be at his prime. His stats probably won't improve beyond much from what we have seen over the past 4 years. His statistics playing with LeBron when they were winning a championship was one of his least productive seasons during his career.

Kevin Love

Season	Team	Games	FG%	3p%	FT%	TRB	AST	STL	PTS
2008-09	MIN	81	.459	.105	.789	9.1	1.0	0.4	11.1
2009-10	MIN	60	.450	.330	.815	11.0	2.3	0.7	14.0
2010-11	MIN	73	.470	.417	.850	15.2	2.5	0.6	20.2
2011-12	MIN	55	.448	.372	.824	13.3	2.0	0.9	26.0
2012-13	MIN	18	.352	.217	.704	14.0	2.3	0.7	18.3
2013-14	MIN	77	.457	.376	.821	12.5	4.4	0.8	26.1
2014-15	CLE	75	.434	.367	.804	9.7	2.2	0.7	16.4
2015-16	CLE	77	.419	.360	.822	9.9	2.4	0.8	16.0
2016-17	CLE	60	.427	.373	.871	11.1	1.9	0.9	19.0
2017-18	CLE	59	.458	.415	.880	9.3	1.7	0.7	17.6
2018-19	CLE	22	.385	.361	.904	10.9	2.2	0.3	17.0
2019-20	CLE	56	.450	.374	.854	9.8	3.2	0.6	17.6

Kevin Love was an all star in Minnesota. He was averaging more points, rebounds, and assists while playing for the Minnesota Timberwolves. In Cleveland his numbers declined. He went from averaging 19.28 points per game with the Minnesota Timberwolves to averaging 17.25 points per game when he teamed with LeBron James from 2015-16 seasons to 2017-18 seasons. Kevin Love had to sacrifice his game, while LeBron has never really had to do that.

Anthony Davis (AD)

Season	Team	Games	FG%	3p%	FT%	TRB	AST	STL	PTS
2012-13	NOH	64	.516	.000	.751	8.2	1.0	1.2	13.5
2013-14	NOP	67	.519	.222	.791	10.0	1.6	1.3	20.8
2014-15	NOP	68	.535	.083	.805	10.2	2.2	1.5	24.4
2015-16	NOP	61	.493	.324	.758	10.3	1.9	1.3	24.3
2016-17	NOP	75	.505	.299	.802	11.8	2.1	1.3	28.0
2017-18	NOP	75	.534	.340	.828	11.1	2.3	1.5	28.1
2018-19	NOP	56	.517	.331	.794	12.0	3.9	1.6	25.9
2019-20	LAL	62	.503	.330	.846	9.3	3.2	1.5	26.1

A myth in the sports talk shows is LeBron made AD better, but truth is he was putting up these great numbers since his time in New Orleans. He was just running into the same problem Jordan and LeBron both faced early in their careers, he had no help with him to get past stronger opponents in the Western Conference. LeBron did not make AD better. While playing in New Orleans, Anthony Davis averaged more rebounds and points, plus his field goal percentage was better. His steals have remain consistent during the course of his career thus far. The areas of improvement in playing with LeBron James was his free throw percentage went up slightly. Overall LeBron has made Anthony Davis shine but he hasn't made him a better player.

Kentavious Caldwall-Pope (KCP)

Season	Team	Games	FG%	3p%	FT%	TRB	AST	STL	PTS
2013-14	DET	80	.396	.319	.770	2.0	0.7	0.9	5.9
2014-15	DET	82	.401	.345	.696	3.1	1.3	1.1	12.7
2015-16	DET	76	.420	.309	.811	3.7	1.8	1.4	14.5
2016-17	DET	76	.399	.350	.832	3.3	2.5	1.2	13.8
2017-18	LAL	74	.426	.383	.789	5.2	2.2	1.4	13.4
2018-19	LAL	82	.430	.347	.867	2.9	2.9	0.9	11.4
2019-20	LAL	69	.467	.385	.775	2.1	2.1	0.8	9.3

KCP in his two seasons with LeBron he has declined in his stat line. He averaged less Rebounds, steals and points per game when he has played with the Lakers and LeBron. He has been consistent with his blocks per game since he came into the league with 0.2. He did average more assists in the 2018-19 campaign where the Lakers failed to reach the playoffs. When he played in Detroit and his first year with the Lakers, he was averaging more points. His points per game declined when LeBron joined the Lakers. KCP also has more seasons where he has played 82 games (2). LeBron James has only done this once in his career.

Kyle Kuzma

Season	Team	Games	FG%	3p%	FT%	TRB	AST	STL	PTS
2017-18	LAL	77	.450	.366	.707	6.3	1.8	0.6	16.1
2018-19	LAL	70	.456	.303	.752	5.5	2.5	0.6	18.7
2019-20	LAL	61	.436	.316	.735	4.5	1.3	0.5	12.8

Kyle Kuzma is a player I enjoy watching. He has been with the Lakers since his rookie season in 2017/18. He started to step up a little in the 2018/19 season and his stats were a little better which is expected for most second year players. This is possibly due to LeBron James getting injured and later sitting out some additional games. By the star Lakers player LeBron James sitting out, this would give Kyle Kuzma and other players more time to be on the court and have more opportunities to get the ball. If you want to claim LeBron makes players better, Kuzma is your best bet, but he has gotten less rebounds per game since teaming with LeBron. His points per game have fluctuated and since he's still early in this career, so it is kind of early to say if LeBron makes him a better scorer or not. Becoming a better scorer just depends if he is able to shoot more and participate more on the offensive side of the ball.

On Christmas day of the 2018-19 season, LeBron was injured from pulling a groin muscle. He was out for 17 games according to CBSsports.com. He then sat out an additional 10 games. Kuzma got more assists and points per game. Is it because LeBron was injured that we got to see a little spike with Kuzma, some games he would be able to put up twenty to over thirty points. In the third year on the Lakers his number started to decline, as he was no longer a starter and was now coming off the bench. This next season will show more of what type of player Kyle Kuzma will become. As they play another season together and Kuzma's numbers could improve more than that his other three seasons, then the argument of LeBron making him better could become valid. But as of now, he pretty much has stayed consistent with what he produces each season, his steals and blocks have stayed about the same.

Nick Wright stated right after the Miami Heat lost the championship in 2020 that Jimmy Butler's legacy was hurt because he lost the championship. In Response I am throwing this out there. Jimmy Butler's legacy was not hurt by losing the championship. Unless Nick is putting Jimmy Butler into the GOAT debate, then he is right. In regards to Kyle Kuzma and his legacy, Kyle Kuzma is 1-0 in the finals as of 2020. That is something LeBron James could never claim, and Kuzma is not in any goat debates...yet!

Argument 18: Is Klutch Sports tampering with the NBA and the Lakers?

Bleacher Report Rob Goldberg wrote an article that questions if Rich Paul is tampering and other agents in the NBA are saying that he is. He quoted in the article of an agent saying "That's the only disappointment is LeBron has leveraged his popularity with young players for seducing them for Klutch and it's not services all the players well." NBA Agent Calls out LeBron James, Rich Paul's Handling of Klutch Sports Athletes, Rob Goldberg, Bleacher Report,

First let's look at what tampering in the NBA is. Tampering within the NBA refers to players, coaches and the front office executives for enticing players who are under contract to play for their franchise (New York Times). In the past couple of years we saw the Lakers President of Basketball Operations Magic Johnson violate this, as well as the Milwaukee Bucks doing the same thing the previous season in regards to their own star Giannis Antetokounmpo on receiving a max contract. All three levels in a basketball organization have to watch what they say when it comes to the stars around the league.

We see LeBron get caught up in this and the media blows it up saying he's trying to tamper by talking about another star. Which is ridiculous. Back in the 90's we saw players being asked about other stars around the league, and it was never considered tampering when Scottie Pippen said Charles Barkley is a good player. Or Jordan being asked what he thought of stars he was completing against. Players will recognize that other players have talent. It's natural because that is their world. They live and breathe their sport, even if they may not like it.

Bill Russell is quoted as once saying "Basketball is what I do, it's not what I am." This means that they are more than what we see on the basketball court.

LeBron James has often said he's "more than an athlete." He doesn't want his basketball career be the only thing about him; he wants to make a difference outside of basketball. He is similar to Bill Russell in this sense. Yet the media members will try to trap him. Media members will ask him questions that they know very well, if he's not careful could get him in trouble for tampering. He knows this, that's why when asked if he would like to play with other stars, in short answer is yes. He and every athlete want to play with top stars. Why? It helps them have to have a better chance in winning. The thing is he's not allowed to flat out say 'Hey, my friend over at team A needs to come play with me.' That would be tampering. I have not seen him tampering, but I find it discouraging that reporters try to bait him. It could be construed as tampering in one interview he had where a reported asked if he would like to play with some other stars. He challenged by saying "Ask me if I would like to play with..." then he mentioned several NBA stars. He answered the question honestly, from what I could tell.

There is a thing in the league called the Bird rights. "The Bird exception, named after Larry Bird, is a rule included in the NBA's Collective Bargaining Agreement that allows a team to go over the salary cap to re-sign their own players. A player qualifies for the Bird Exception, formally referred to as a Qualifying Veteran Free Agent, is said to have the 'Bird rights'." Hoops Rumors. This basically means that when a team wants to keep a player they can go over the salary cap to keep their own player.

With this in mind, let's finish this argument about Klutch Sports. Is Klutch Sports tampering in the NBA? I have not seen any reason to believe they are. However it does rise suspicion that

LeBron James best friend Rich Paul who is the CEO of Klutch Sports, has numerous clients that all seem to have an association with signing with the team LeBron is on, currently bringing these big name players to the Lakers. Now as of last season around ½ of the Lakers roster were Klutch Sports clients.

In the championship season 2019/20 Klutch Sports clients on the Lakers included LeBron James, Anthony Davis, J.R. Smith, Kentavious Caldwell-Pope, Dion Waiters, Markieff Morris, and Talen Horton-Tucker.

For the 2020/21 season Klutch Sports clients include LeBron James, Anthony Davis, J. R. Smith, Kentavious Caldwell-Pope, Dion Waiters, Markieff Morris, Talen Horton Tucker and Montrezl Harrell. A way to work around talking to players is through agents. This could be why ½ of the Lakers roster are all under the same Agent.

In previous seasons, why did no big name free agents like Carmelo Anthony, Kawhi Leonard, Kevin Durant or Chris Paul not sign on to play with LeBron James? I would imagine that there would be players lined up around the league to want to play with him, after all, who wouldn't want to play with the best player on the planet? Yet for 16 years no major superstar would come to play with him? He has had to run to Miami to play with other superstars like Dwayne Wade and Chris Bosh. Then go to the Los Angeles Lakers for him to bring other stars like Another Davis to play? Even in his first year in LA no one was coming. It wasn't until Anthony Davis had Rich Paul talking to him that suddenly he wanted to play in LA. So it is tampering when the agent is the one recruiting and talking to players around the league? Should an agent be influencing his clients on where they should play? That's something I cannot answer, but how else do the Lakers get Anthony Davis without Rich Paul and LeBron James in his ear?

Argument 19: Jordon won once the Pistons and Celtics got Old

I hear argument a lot from none other than Nick Wright on First Things First, as a way to say Michael Jordan only won a championship because everyone else was either too old to beat him or too young. This is absurd.

The average age of the pistons roster in the 1989/90 season was 29 years old. The Pistons are two time NBA champions at the end of this season with Isiah Thomas getting Finals MVP. The Detroit Pistons at this point were in the championship three years in a row. The average age of the Chicago Bulls in this same season was 26.21 years old. So were the Pistons only winning because the Bulls were too Young?

The average age for the Detroit Pistons in 1990/91 season is 30.64 years old. The average age of the Chicago Bulls Roster in the same season was 26.58 years old. The Pistons were champions for the previous two seasons and were trying to reach the finals for the fourth year. The Pistons did not get too old, when they are defending champions. We never say that the Pistons only won because the Lakers and Celtics were too old. It's like saying the Spurs were too old when they lost in 2013, when their average ago of their roster was 27.8 years old. The truth is the Bulls beat a primed Detroit Pistons team and the Detroit Pistons never recovered from that defeat. Jordan never got over the physicality that the Pistons did purposely to him. That's why Isiah Thomas and Michael Jordan remain bitter towards each other to this day.

The Chicago Bulls roster in 1998 had an average age of 29.47 years old; this was in their last season winning the championship. Yet four of their core starters were all over 30 years old. Ron Harper (34), Tony Kukoc (29), Michael Jordan (34), Scottie Pippen (32), and Dennis Rodman (36) average ages was 33. By today's standards this team would be considered too old to win a championship. The 1991 Pistons Starting line-up included Joe Dumars (27), Isiah Thomas (29), Bill Laimbeer (33), Dennis Rodman (29), and James Edwards (35), whose average age were 30.6. The 91 Pistons starters were younger than the 98 Bulls starting lineup. Like I stated before, it is not true that a team who had won the championship the previous two years was now too old. They were in their prime, the Bulls were also in their prime and the better team won. These things are left out of discussions of the Pistons/Bulls segments because it shows Jordan beating a great team and he overcame them. The Pistons walked off the court once they knew they were not going to win. It appears too many including myself that the Detroit Pistons forfeited with only seconds remaining.

As far as the Celtics are concerned, Jordan didn't play the Celtics again in the playoffs during the rest of the 80's. So claiming he only got past them because they got old is not valid because he did not play them beyond his third season. It's a hypothetical argument and there is no room for hypothetical's.

I also have also seen Nick Wright say Michael Jordan never beat Larry Bird, and that is true. What he doesn't mention is the Jordan/Bird playoff battles were only occurred twice in their careers the 1985/86 and 1986/87 playoffs. The next time Michael Jordan would see Larry Bird on the opposing team was when Larry Bird was a head coach for the Indiana Pacers. When Larry Bird was a head coach, Michael Jordan did beat the Indiana Pacers. I never understood why Nick Wright tries to use this argument that Larry Bird and the Celtics got old and that's when Michael Jordon started winning championships. The Celtics getting old should not go against Michael Jordan. It should go against

Isiah Thomas and the Detroit Pistons. If Larry Bird and the Celtics were too old, isn't that why the Detroit Pistons won their championships? I'm just saying...

To say Jordan only won because a team was too old is insulting. If a 30 year old pistons team was too old, what's the excuse for the San Antonio team that was 27 years old that LeBron beat in 2013? Didn't that San Antonio Spurs team come back the year after to defeat the Miami Heat? Wouldn't the San Antonio Spurs be older? I see the excuse from Skip Bayless that LeBron James beat an old Tim Duncan. Tim Duncan got revenge the following season with a championship. I don't put the Sam Antonio Spurs team that lost to the Miami Heat as old. I don't put the Detroit Pistons as old because like I said, they were back to back champions and simply got outplayed in the 1991 playoffs against the Chicago Bulls to get swept four games to none.

Argument 20: the eye test

I decided to add the eye test because it's often said LeBron is the best basketball player Nick Wright has ever seen. When comparing the two, I will say we are comparing apples to oranges. Why? We are watching two athletes whose play styles are completely different. The on air personalities that use the eye test are Cris Carter, Skip Bayless, Max Kellerman and Chris Broussard.

LeBron: He is a physical specimen that we haven't seen very often in sports in general, especially in basketball. His build and play style is closer to that of Magic Johnson. He loves to facilitate the offense and has no problem passing the ball late in the game. Since this is a book, I can't show any highlights. However, all you have to do is YouTube and you can see some of the highlights and his best plays of his career. These videos are made mainly by fans. He is also an incredible passer, the best since Magic Johnson and Larry Bird. He can jump extremely high, or it appears that way since his hands can reach the top of the backboard.

Jordan: Jordan is different from LeBron, much different. Jordan had this unique ability where he and the defender would jump at the exact same time and when the defender would be losing altitude, Jordan is still going up. He had incredible strength, endurance, and technical abilities that could not be matched, even by Kobe. He was able to do what I can only describe as trick shots, no look shots/layups. He had a nearly un-blockable fade away shot. Playing matches whether it be exhibition or a real regular season/playoff game he would show off his different arsenal of dunks to entertain and amp up the crowd. He was able to make free throws with his eyes closed, and there are videos of him doing those free throws. Jordan was just incredible to watch. If you have not seen Jordan actually play here are some things you can do. YouTube the *Bulls Threepeat Documentary*, Netflix *The Last Dance* documentary, or Amazon Prime *Ultimate Jordan: Come Fly with Me*. You can also look up his highlights or simply watch ESPN or any Fox Sports segments where they talk about Jordan.

Argument 21: Underachieving

I do not see the media talking about LeBron James or Michael Jordan for underachieving. So I decided to include it as one of the arguments.

I don't have to look far with LeBron James, he has been swept in the finals twice (2007, 2018). He had a gentlemens sweep against him in 2017. He has the 2011 lost to the Mavericks who did the unthinkable and won with only 1 All star on the team. This should have not been possible, and it wasn't done by either LeBron or Jordan. It was done by Dirk Nowitzki. This 2011 loss LeBron had a meltdown on the basketball court. Believe it or not it's a blemish on LeBron because it showed he wasn't mentally ready for this type of stage. To make matters worse for him, he wasn't even the best player on the Heat that season, Dwayne Wade was. Wade being the best player on the Heat is often left out of Jordan/LeBron goat debates. LeBron went 9 seasons before he won his first championship. When we talk about many of the other greats, they won sooner. Magic Johnson and Bill Russell both won in their first year in the league. Kareem Abdul-Jabbar won with Milwaukee in his second season. Shaq and Wilt Chamberlain both won their first title in their 8th year in the league. Michael Jordan won his first title in his 7th year in the league. Kobe Bryant won his first title in his fourth year in the league.

Michael Jordan underachieved in not getting past the first round of the playoffs during the early years of his career. He also has some people saying that the Wizards years he underachieved because they didn't make the playoffs those two years. While I did go over the first round exits, it should not be considered underachieving when he did help his team make the playoffs. However, for the GOAT debate, others did win the championship sooner than Michael Jordan.

Will LeBron win more championships? I believe he will, he has his agent to help bring in more talent to the team he's on. Plus with the additions they made for the 2020/21 season, Lakers are the heavy favorites to repeat the championship for the 2020/21 NBA season.

Argument 22: Who is More Clutch?

I have seen this argument on both ESPN and Fox Sports. All of the shows debate this and I will give credit to both networks for this one. All of the TV show analysts have talked about who is more clutch.

Jordan is 9-18: 50% in clutch moments. Buzzer Beaters 3.

LeBron 10-27: 37% in clutch moments. Buzzer Beaters 4.

While some numbers will suggest LeBron is more clutch, it is widely more accepted that Michael Jordan, Kobe Bryant, Paul Pierce, Reggie Miller are more clutch and are the type of players a team will go to in taking the last shot. LeBron has stats to stay he has done it more, but he has not done it better. This is part of the longevity argument. It also says LeBron has been in more situations of close games compared to Jordan or Kobe. This is often debated on EPSN and Fox Sport talk shows. Who do you put as the more clutch performer? LeBron James or Michael Jordan? Statistics for the clutch moments were found on ESPN and insidehoops.com

Let's look at the LeBron James, Kobe Bryant and Michael Jordan when it comes to their records at facing teams that won 50+ games and 60 + games.

	50+ Win Teams	60+Win Teams
Kobe	25-10	2-5
MJ	20-7	7-2
LeBron	10-9	3-4

Argument 23: Analytics

This argument I see Nick Wright push because he's an analytics guy on the Fox Sports show First Things First. He loves talking about numbers and he will put all kinks of lists up that most of the fans don't fully understand. He would make most of us believe that LeBron is a far superior player and almost every single stat that he puts up always favors LeBron. With that said, do you remember how I have stated that Fox Sports TV hosts push for that LeBron as the GOAT narrative, and things are omitted on purpose?

Analytics have several categories. The concept of the analytics was designed by John Hollinger where he used mathematics to "determine the worth of a player is both over-valuing AND devaluing a player at the same time" (William Johnson, Bleacher Report).

The following is from BasketballReference.com. In looking up these stats, there are many miss leading and old data that could confuse the average fan. It is often used that before John Hollinger redid his formula that players like LeBron James and Russell Westbrook ran away with some of these stats. After a few improvements it has placed Michael Jordan at the top of these analytics.

Value over Replacement rankings

1. Michael Jordan at 12.47. 1987-88
2. LeBron James at 11.79. 2008-09.
3. Michael Jordan at 11.42. 1988-89

Jordan holds 6 of the top 10 VOR ratings for the NBA. LeBron holds 2 of the top 10 VOR ratings in the NBA.

Player Efficiency Rating (PER)

1. Michael Jordan at 27.91
2. LeBron James a 27.49
3. Anthony Davis at 27.42.

Box Plus/Minus

1. Michael Jordan 9.22
2. LeBron James: 8.93

Win Shares

1. Kareem Abdul-Jabbar 273.41
2. Wilt Chamberlain 247.26
3. LeBron James 236.44
4. Karl Malone 234.63
5. Michael Jordan 214.02

True Shooting Percentage

45: LeBron James: .5860

97. Michael Jordan: .5686

Usage Percentage

Michael Jordan has 4 separate ratings before LeBron has one. The following list ranks them amongst NBA players in the top 50 rankings.

#5 Michael Jordan 38.29

#14 Michael Jordan 35.99

#33 Michael Jordan 34.71

#44 Michael Jordan 34.06

#46 LeBron James 33.82

#47 Michael Jordan 33.74

#48 Michael Jordan 33.67

In analytics I often see the older analytics used. Rarely do the TV show hosts put up the more updated numbers which more often than not favors Michael Jordan over LeBron James. If these analytic guys were objective, I would see even the LeBron supporters putting up these numbers so fans are being shown facts, and those facts are up to date.

Argument #24: Triple Doubles

I do see all of the different sport talk shows bring up Triple Doubles. They don't really place this in the GOAT debates.

Triple doubles was not something I heard much about growing up. I did not see players openly trying to get triple doubles in games or it being something that was very important. That is not the case today. Players are now more open about saying how they want to be great players over all, not being a player that's only good at one thing. In other words, they don't want to be a one trick pony, which means only good at one thing, or known for one thing. Players like Lonzo Ball, Russell Westbrook and LeBron James are players that try to get the triple doubles. They want to be the triple threat when they are in a game. This way they have optimum opportunities to help their individual team's success.

With that being said, Triple doubles have not been placed as a statistic until 1979. In 1979, it officially started being recorded as a statistic.

As of before the 2020/21 season the top players with Triple Doubles are the following

1. Oscar Robinson – 181
2. Russell Westbrook – 146
3. Magic Johnson – 138
4. Jason Kidd – 107
5. **LeBron James** – 94
    15. **Michael Jordan** – 28

Here are the triple doubles in the playoffs

1. Magic Johnson – 30
2. **LeBron James** – 28
3. Jason Kidd – 11
4. Rajon Rondo – 10
5. Russell Westbrook – 10
6. Draymond Green – 10
7. Larry Bird – 10
8. Wilt Chamberlain – 9
9. Oscar Robinson – 8
    29. **Michael Jordan** – 2

As you can see, Oscar Robinson has dominated the triple doubles during the regular season. But with Russell Westbrook being known to get them as well as LeBron James, it would not be surprising if we see one or both of those players pass Oscar on this list.

LeBron wins the Triple Double argument against Michael Jordan. Jordan was mostly known as a scorer and since he didn't get the assists or rebounds, this category favors LeBron.

Both in the Regular season and in the playoffs LeBron has a clear advantage in having by far more triple doubles during his career compared to Michael Jordan. He is also the first player in NBA history to have triple doubles vs. 30 teams according to NBA.com. The competition he has for triple doubles is from GOAT candidate Magic Johnson, and honorable mention player Russell Westbrook.

Argument #25: Ejections, Foul Outs, turnovers and sitting out

One of the things that shows an impressive resume is if a player has not been fouled out. It's also impressive if a player has never been ejected from a game during the course of their career. The longer the player's career is the more chances that either of these scenarios can occur. Another impressive feat for players is when they play every single game of the season as long as the player is healthy.

FOUL-OUTS and EJECTIONS

According to the Los Angeles Times in an *article No One Dares Foul Up Game* by Jim Murray, "Do you know how many times Wilt Chamberlain fouled out of a game in his career of 1,045 games and 160 in the playoffs? None. Not one."

According to ESPN.com, during Michael Jordan's career he has fouled out of games total of 11 times in his 15 year career. In that time span he has also never been ejected from a basketball game.

LeBron James has fouled out of games 8 times during his 17 year career in the NBA career. He has been ejected once during that time span. The ejection occurred during a game of the Cleveland Cavaliers versus the Miami Heat where Kane Fitzgerald [a referee] called back to back technical fouls on LeBron James after LeBron James voiced his frustrations and he threw a punch in the air. These two things led to the back to back technical fouls that got him ejected from the game. This occurred during the third quarter on November 28, 2017. Articles from the Washington Post, ESPN and Bleacher Report were made after this occurred. This was big news because that is the only time in his career up to the 2019/20 season, which LeBron James was ejected from a basketball game.

Why would foul outs or ejections matter? It matters because it is part of the game. This area of basketball is normally the negative part of the game. It's a part of the game people don't like because as games extend (like the 1993 NBA Finals game 3 when the game went into triple overtime), that the major stars on the team that fans trust to help the team to win can be fouled out and put the win in jeopardy. If a player is ejected early it also can take out the best player on a team or one of their best; and now there can be a void on the team that can't be replaced. We have seen teams struggle without their best player on the court.

TURNOVERS: Turnovers are also another major part of the NBA. Basketballreferance.com has a list of the all time leaders in turnovers. The more turnovers the player has means the more opportunities that are given to the opposition in scoring and/or winning the game. While players like Karl Malone and LeBron James are at the top of the scoring lists they are also at the very top for career turnovers.

Top five in turnovers are

1.	Karl Malone	4,524
2.	**LeBron James**	4,441
3.	Moses Malone	4,264
4.	John Stockton	4,244
5.	Kobe Bryant	4,010

Other GOAT Candidates career turnovers

10.	Hakeem Olajuwon	3,667
14.	Magic Johnson	3,506
20.	Shaquille O'Neal	3,310
33.	**Michael Jordan**	2,924
38.	Larry Bird	2,816
48.	Kevin Durant	2,663
57.	Kareem Abdul-Jabbar	2,527
98.	Stephen Curry	2,196

SITTING OUT GAMES

Michael Jordan has had three seasons in his fifteen year career where he did not play a full season. These are not because he chooses to sit out. In the 1985/86 season he sustained a foot injury during the 8th game of the season. This took him out for most of the season. In the 1994/95 season, he came out of retirement and played 18 games at the end of the regular season. In the 2001/02 season he injured his knee, forcing him to only play 60 games. He was out the remainder of the season.

The other 12 seasons 1984/85, 1986/87, 1987/88, 1988/89, 1989/90, 1990/91, 1991/92, 1992/93, 1995/96, 1996/97, 1997/98, 2002/2003 he played all 82 regular season games.

Michael Jordan has stated in the past that he wanted to play every game because there could be a fan in the seats that has never seen him play before. He wanted to give it his all and show why he was the best player in the world. He has stated this numerous times in his career and even after his career ended. Other media members that have reminded fans about this include Skip Bayless and Chris Broussard.

LeBron James has been in the NBA for 17 years and is now in his 18th season. During the course of his career, he has only played all 82 regular season games once during his career, the 2017/18 season.

LeBron has had other seasons where he played a majority of the season.

2004/05: 80 games.

2008/09: 81 games.

He's had ten seasons where he's had 70 or more games played.

He's had three seasons where he's had 60 or more games played.

He's had one season where he's played 50 or more games. 55 games played in 2018/19 due to injury, he sat out 17 games due to injury and then an additional 10 games).

Two seasons of his career were shorten seasons. The 2019/20 season was cut short due to a worldwide COVID19 pandemic. The 2011/12 season was a shorten season in the NBA because of almost two months of inactivity and negotiations between the players and the NBA. Those two seasons of course cannot be held against LeBron James when the league doesn't have all 82 games.

Argument #26: Michael Jordan and the Washington Wizards years

In this section I believe Chris Broussard from Fox Sports gives the best argument for the years that Michael Jordan played with the Washington Wizards. For most of this I got the information from Fox Sports with a video from Chris Broussard discussing Michael Jordan's years with the Washington Wizards.

Chris Broussard stated "He dropped 51 points against the Hornets. He became the oldest player in NBA history to score at least 40 points in a game. He scored a game winner against the Knicks in Madison Square Garden. I'm not talking about MJ in Chicago, I'm talking about MJ in Washington, because you kids just don't know how good Michael Jordan was with the Wizards."

"I hear this all the time, he tarnished his legacy, he ruined the perfect story book ending. Jordan should have never unretired again and played for the Wizards...This Notion that he put a blemish on his career over his last two years in Washington is the biggest misconceptions in all of basketball. Here's why.

#1: Jordan's stats in Washington were legit

Legitimate All-Star. All NBA type of numbers."

Season	Team	Games	FG%	3p%	FT%	TRB	AST	STL	PTS
2001-02	WAS	60	.416	.189	.790	5.7	5.2	1.4	22.9
2002-03	WAS	82	.445	0291	.821	6.1	3.8	1.5	20.0

Chris Broussard in the same video goes on to say "In his first season with the Wizards 2001-2002 he averaged more than 22 points, more than 5 rebounds and more than 5 assists a game... His second season 428 players took the floor that year. Of those 428 only 11 averaged at least 20 points, 6 rebounds and 3.5 assists a game. Michael Jordan was one of them. One of eleven, at age 40. He also had nine games where he scored 30 or more points. That's more than Chris Webber, more than Gary Payton, More than Vince Carter. He also dropped 40 or more three times, more than Dirk Nowitzki and Ray Allen that year. So at age 40 Jordan was out performing hall of famers and perennial All-Stars who were in their primes."

"In his two years in Washington Jordan had 8 games where had 40 or more points while he was shooting at least 50% from the field. To put that into perspective Hall of Famer Chris Mullen has 7 such games in his career. Hall Of Famers Reggie Miller and Mitch Richmond had 9 such games in their careers. Two of the best swing men in the league today Kawhi Leonard has 6 and Jimmy Butler has 5 in their careers."

#2 Clutch Moments

Chris Broussard goes on to talk about game winning moments where Jordan takes game winning shots. Some games he mentions are against the New York Knicks, The New Jersey Nets and Cleveland Cavaliers. I won't go into those, just know he made the clutch shots in those games. To see more details please look up Fox Sports YouTube video of Chris Broussard "Michael Jordan on the Wizards". He also goes over the All Star game in the clutch moments.

#3 Wizards improved with Jordan on the court

"Contrary to popular opinion the Wizards actually improved a great deal with Jordan on the court. The year before he joined the Wizards, they won 19 games. That was Third worst in the NBA. Jordan's first season with the Wizards were limited to 60 games because to a knee injury. But they went 30-30 in those games." Stated Chris Broussard. He also mentions how Jordan in the month of January scored more points per game in the month of January that the league's MVP for that season Tim Duncan.

I love listening and watching Chris Broussard. I feel he is very objective and is fair in voting for the NBA's Most Valuable Player, scoring titles, defensive player of the year, etc. He has his favorite players and teams but talks about the players in a fair way. He will say if some other player is doing better, like Anthony Davis putting up better statistics than LeBron James.

In the Michael Jordan versus LeBron James GOAT debates, he puts up great arguments for both Michael Jordan and LeBron James. That's something that no other sports analysts has done in the past five years, that I could find.

Michael Jordan holds the record for the oldest league player to be in the All Star game at 39 years old, just shy of turning 40 years old. Like Chris Broussard said, he didn't get the All Star game because of his name, but because he earned that spot.

TOPICS

This next section contains weaker arguments and I do not include them in real debates, but since social media and sports talk shows bring these topics up, I am listing some of them. These arguments to me show no validity because it has little or no value in the actual game of basketball. These topics are mainly from off the basketball court undertakings made by players. Often I see these topics used when people run out of arguments on who they claim as the GOAT.

Topic 1: Activist impacts

LeBron: Mainly known for his social activism he speaks on social issues that include Black Lives Matters, Cops relations with the black community, etc. He has spoken up and confronted President Donald Trump. Their interactions on social media are entertaining to say the least. The only social activist movement that goes against LeBron is when he didn't speak up to support freedoms in Hong Kong, China. This mainly occurred back in the end of 2019 and was a result of then, Houston Rockets General Manager Daryl Morey making a comment on Twitter that the people of Hong Kong should be free.

LeBron responded by saying "Yes we all do have freedoms of speech, but at times there are ramifications, for the negative that can happen when you're not thinking about others, you're only thinking of yourself. So I don't believe, I don't want to get into word, or sentence a feud with Daryl, with Daryl Morey. But I believe he wasn't educated on, on the situation at hand. And um he Spoke. And So many people could have been harmed, not only financially but physically, emotionally, spiritually. So just be careful on what we tweet and what we say. Or what we do. Even though yes we have freedom of speech" (October 2019).

He lost credibility from the sports talk shows and even the public when the situation with China came out. In America it is easy to stand behind any movement because there are little to no ramifications that come with it. With China it's different for LeBron. Why? How? It is because LeBron has business interests in China. His Nike shoes are made out there, he makes money out there. So if China refuses to make or sell his merchandise, he can lose millions of dollars. So when here is a chance to really show his passion and to really stand up for people who really are oppressed, he did not take the opportunity to embrace the world activism which would put him on the level of Mohammad Ali. Instead when it came to him speaking out against oppression that is abroad, where he has business interests. He literally just *shut up and dribbled* and he told Daryl Morey to *shut up and general manage.* Radio hosts like Clay Travis go over their interpretation of the events that took place stating similar to what I just said.

Does this take away from LeBron James on the political activism in America? No it doesn't. It takes more than an isolated event taking place on the other side of the world to take away from everything he has done here in America. He has been active in his communities and above all telling the Black community to be proud and stay united. He tells his followers and the media that being black is a life style. He also has helped with things like improving education for poor black children, and encouraging the masses to go out and vote. His overall impact outside of basketball has helped him gain respect amongst the public and NBA fans. He is able to use his many platforms to help spread awareness on many social issues.

Jordan: Many people during Jordan's NBA career wanted Jordan to be Like Mohammad Ali, they wanted him to speak up for the Black community, and he never did. He had a chance to support Harvey Gantt who was running for the US Senate back in 1990 against Jesse Helms. Many in the black community wanted him to speak out and give a public endorsement to Harvey Gantt. They wanted him to do a commercial to show support. Jordan instead gave a statement on a bus ride with his teammates "Republican's buy sneakers too." (Last Dance Episode 5). Jordan gave Gantt a contribution which is often ignored. Jordan has felt he has not had to correct this sneakers comment and in the documentary he stated "I don't think that statement needs to be corrected because I said it in jess on a bus with Horace Grant and Scottie Pippen and it was thrown off the cuff."

Jordan since his retirement from basketball, he has become a team owner with the Charlotte Hornets. He is the first player/Owner to reach a status of becoming a Billionaire. He has made donations to several charities in his local community in North Carolina. He has helped in funding two hospitals to be built for families that cannot afford health insurance. He has pledged to donate $100 million dollars to support the Black Lives Matter movement over the next ten years.

The differences between Jordan/LeBron; is LeBron is more vocal on off the court topics compared to when Jordan was playing. I see these topics of activism, LeBron's "I Promise School" and Jordan with his hospital and donations once the two sides run out of area's to cover in their goat debates. Off the court things like this is something that should not be in real GOAT debates. I say this because you don't see every great player being advocates in different movements. It's a choice of the player, and to say LeBron deserves to get more praise than Jordan is not valid. When we talk about the greatest of all time, we are talking about what that player has accomplished on the basketball court.

If we were to say off the court things should be a part of it then include it in all player contracts, let players know they can never be considered the best if they are not a part of an activist movement of some sorts. So unfortunately, I cannot say these things have any validity when it comes to GOAT debates. However, I do give commends to LeBron for his activism.

Topic 2: Media Platforms

LeBron is building his own brand, he's using different media platforms, and he has his own HBO show called "The Shop" where all of the guests that appear on the show agree with anything this man says. It's not like a real barber shop where they all openly debate on different topics. While I could list guests and topics they discuss, maybe I'll save that for a future book, if I decide to write it. He even has opened up about the GOAT debates to ESPN More than an Athlete where "James reflected on winning the 2016 NBA Championship with the Cleveland Cavaliers, in which they overcame a 3-1 deficit against the Golden State Warriors" Business Insider Scott Davis, LeBron James says he knew he was the greatest NBA player of all-time after helping the Cavs win a championship. James goes on to say in the show that "That one right there made me the greatest player of all-time, that's what I felt."

Is it right for LeBron to say he's the greatest of all time? Of course it's okay for him to say it. I tell my own children they are great, I tell them to tell themselves they are great at anything they want to be the best at. It's that drive and passion that will help them in believing they can achieve anything. So LeBron can say that to himself but the difference is he said that not just to himself, he said it to the world. Many people take it as LeBron James is not humble, due to this it's used against him.

Michael Jordan has not come out to flat out say he's the greatest of all time. He has hinted at it, but has never officially said he's the greatest ever. When he's been asked about it, I'll paraphrase... he has said you can't compare different eras. He didn't get to play against all of the greatest players that were before him. He lets the media talk and talk and talk about it. I guess that works because the media talks about it every day, even on days when the shows are not live. You see the debates persisting.

Both Jordan and LeBron have taken advantage of their status in basketball and have made movies. Jordan helped jumpstart basketball movies by filming Space Jam at the conclusion of the 95 season. He had his friends like Charles Barkley, Larry Bird, Patrick Ewing get cameos. He even had a practice facility built on set for him to practice so he can prepare for the 1995/96 NBA season. Jordan has been in several commercials, documentaries and has appeared in a couple of movies like Goat Camp (short in 2020), Looney Tunes Back in Action. He has had a couple of documentaries like The Last Dance, The Bulls Three Peat, Untouchabulls. One thing I find interesting is his shoes of Jordan 13 was in the Spike Lee movie He Got Game starring Denzel Washington and Ray Allen. I have never seen a shoe being brought up as a fact or special feature of a movie, but in this case it made a 20 year anniversary in 2018 when NIKE re-released the shoe due to the movie.

Topic 3: Gambling

I have seen this on Undisputed a few times but they don't really go into a lot of details, it mainly was covered because of the Last Dance Documentary. In the documentary Michael Jordan discusses how he gambled and that it wasn't a problem. This got ESPN and Fox Sports to jump on this subject and discuss it due to an episode. Since there were no sports taking place at the time due to the pandemic shutting down most sports, this was the most this has been talked about since the 1990s.

This topic is not about LeBron, it's about Michael Jordan. People try to claim that his addiction to gambling was so severe that it led to his dad getting killed over his gambling debts. That is all conspiracy non sense. His dad was not killed by anyone linked to gambling sharks. His dad was killed by a couple of kids that had a robbery gone wrong. There has never been any evidence to support the gambling Michael did have had anything to do with his father's death. With that said, they also say that because he spent hundreds of thousands of dollars on gambling due to checks coming out that he had a problem. Did he have a gambling problem? I don't know, I wasn't there. I can say that I have not seen any evidence to say that he gambled on any outcome of his own games, like we are going to lose Game 1. He didn't do that, but what he did gamble on was his golf game. He would bet on card games, and would have these games with his friends, his inner circle, his teammates, and other players around the league.

The truth is everyone gambles, even if it's not widely known. Most people however will not gamble thousands of dollars. They will keep it low and friendly, like $1 for a hand. Or they will say to their friends I got $20 that says the Patriots win the next game. I know a lot of people who play the Lottery. Guess what, the lotto is a form of gambling.

The other thing with the gambling is it leads to the next conspiracy of Jordan's first retirement is a secret suspension. I would believe this if Jordan wasn't talking about retirement after his second championship. The reason he didn't retire is he wanted to do what Larry and Magic never did, win three in a row (Last Dance Documentary). When I was growing up, it disappointed me greatly that he retired. I was in fourth grade when he retired, and I actually wrote a story about the Bull's having a second threepeat. No one thought that would happen. The teacher asked me why I didn't have them win 4 in a row, I said "Because they don't have Mike." I had in my story Pippen becoming the teams Leader and he took the team on his back and he would lead them to three more championships. I guess looking back it was an entertaining story.

The retirement of Michael Jordan was shocking to everyone. Fans of the Bulls and Jordan never wanted to see him step away from the game of basketball. I was not able to find anything to support that the NBA was going to suspend Jordan for the gambling investigation. Though the conspiracy will live on.

Just like Media and Activism I see the gambling brought up to say someone doesn't respect Jordan's life style and choices he made. It doesn't in any way say Jordan wasn't the greatest basketball player to ever play the game. Is he the greatest gambler ever? You can debate that.

Topic 4: Personal Life

This is again something that has nothing to do with what Michael Jordan and LeBron James do on the basketball court. I wouldn't even bring this up if I didn't see it used in live chats. But here it goes; it will be quick and short.

Michael Jordan divorced his wife Juanita Jordan who he has two sons with. In the divorce settlement it hit a record $168 million dollars. The divorce was a result of "Jordan's gambling addiction and cheating ways" (Bleacher Report "Don't Confuse Greatness with Class: Why Michael Jordan Is No DiMaggio" by Benny Vargas, July 21, 2010). It's speculated that he paid people hush money to have affairs but as I looked around I did not see much to support this. Most of what I found is rumors and regardless of the speculations, it is a fact that they divorced.

LeBron James has a better off court image; he is a good father that interacts beautifully with his wife and children. Have you seen videos of him with his daughter? Adorable! He has never been questioned as being a good man outside the game of basketball...or has he?

It has been speculated that he had an affair with an IG model. According to *The Fumble*, Sophia Jhamora has been seen courtside of Lakers games and she is linked to LeBron and some of his teammates like Kyle Kuzma. This is all speculation and rumors, but it has gained popularity in these live chats where people try to use player's personal lives against them. During a YouTube video *The Fumble* also suggested that he has reached out to several women in IG. He uses the direct message feature to talk to women. The DM or texts were never addressed by LeBron according to *The Fumble*.

These are rumors. I don't like putting this type of nonsense in GOAT debates. I couldn't care less about how these men are outside the game of basketball. I'm writing about who's the greatest basketball player, not who's the best husband or father.

It is used as I said in live chats. Would you use this in your own GOAT debates as to say this is why Michael Jordan or LeBron James are NOT the GOAT? Is it credible when talking basketball? Have you ever cheated on someone you're in a relationship with or were with? You can answer those questions.

Topic 5: Spending Habits

On some TV sports shows on ESPN and Fox Sports, LeBron James is said to spend over a million dollars every year to keep his mind and body in top condition. He makes sure he and his family is eating the right foods, he is getting the exercise he needs and he pays for it. People say anyone can do this, but I have not been able to spend a million dollars every year for getting nutritionists and trainers to keep me in top health. I wish I had that kind of money. LeBron has to be given credit for taking his health very seriously. If more athletes did this imagine how many more stars would play longer in the NBA and other sports. Maybe we would see cities like San Diego, CA; Birmingham, AL; Nashville, TN get some expansion teams? It would be exciting to see more teams added to the NBA based on more players taking better care of themselves and thus getting more teams as more players are drafted into the NBA.

James also has used his money to branch outside of basketball. He has created his own media empire. He has his HBO specials and movie deals. He is staring in an upcoming Space Jam 2, sequel to the Michael Jordan Space Jam? He has been praised for being a teammate that spends money on team events and activities. He gives his teammates gifts and brings them together. This is something that players have talked about and is rarely a subject mentioned during sports talk shows. It has been on the shows, but segments are very brief. I mainly have seen this on Undisputed on Fox Sports FS1.

Michael Jordan: While he played basketball, he made $126 million during his career. That is nothing compared to today's players. For comparison, LeBron has a 4 year $154 million dollar deal with the L.A. Lakers. Jordan has Nike's Jordan brand which continues to bring in significant income with $4.2 billion yearly. He is the richest former professional athlete in history, and is ranked 455th richest person in America (Boss Hunting). As I said earlier Jordan pledged to donate $100 million dollars to racial quality and social justice and greater access to education. He has donated $2.8 million for Hurricane Florence Relief efforts and undisclosed amounts to the NAACP Legal Defense Fund and the International Association of Chiefs of Police's Institute for Community-Police Relations. Jordan has spent his money on several restaurants. He has a Nissan dealership in Durham, North Carolina. He also has spent money on several cars like Mercedes and Pontiacs. He also has Ferrari 512 TR, Porsche 911 and an Aston Martin DB7 Volante. Unlike LeBron, I didn't find anything to say he spent money on his teammates when he was a player.

I often wonder why people care about what these guys spend their money on. It is strange to me, that some people do care. Their spending has not helped me in any way so I do not care what they spend their money on. I also don't think that it should not matter if they spend their money on teammates or not. Teammates don't always spend money on them. Plus if LeBron was to retire, considering he doesn't like to tell people his future plans, it seems unlikely that he will tell everyone when his farewell season will be. So if he keeps his retirement plans in the hush, hush, then it would make it so his teammates are not likely to get him a farewell present. Jordan didn't get any farewell presents on any retirement. He would just retire and it was always unknown what his plans were as well.

Topic 6 Media and the Fans

This is the last topic I will cover before giving my final analysis on who is the undisputed GOAT. Remember earlier how I said it is the fans of LeBron that causes the disrespect he receives? While I don't like to name people directly, Nick Wright has gone on social media and will consistently belittle and irate about players like Kobe Bryant and Michael Jordan to try and discredit them as the GOAT. When you are in the media, especially when you are being broadcasted to millions of people's homes, you should be objective. This is because someone may be watching your show for the first time ever. That person may not know sports, may not know basketball, or not have had a chance to watch the previous all time greats play. With that said, there is no need to attack a player's legacy in order to boost another player like LeBron James. His body of work should be able to speak for itself.

The day before Kobe Bryant Died, Kobe congratulated LeBron James on passing him on the all time scoring leaders list on Twitter. This is an amazing accomplishment and just as Kobe gave LeBron praise for this achievement, Nick Wright sent out a tweet stating the following. "Now that LeBron has more career points that Kobe, he officially leads him in the following categories in the regular season and playoffs: Points Rebounds Assists Blocks Steals PPG RPG APG FG% 3FG% PER TS% Win Shares VORP BOM MVPs Finals MVPs. Kobe was a better FT shooter, tho." This was taken by many as disrespectful. This is a moment to congratulate LeBron on an incredible milestone in his career. Instead Nick belittles Kobe's career. While he may have just wanted to point out that LeBron leads in several categories, he should not have used that moment to talk down about Kobe's career. It wasn't until after Kobe Bryant died the following day that Nick Wright finally said kind words about Kobe. It wasn't until Kobe died that he finally realized the impact that Kobe had on basketball, on fans, on Los Angeles, and around the world. If he truly is a fan of basketball, he would have already understood the greatness of Kobe, and not take shots at him for years. Like I stated before, its media and LeBron fanatics like Nick Wright that make other fans lose respect towards LeBron. For making GOAT arguments, please instead of having to degrade, belittle, trash talk other players, list the things like stats, advance stats, accolades, and records to build your case.

The tweet Nick Wright put out on January 25, 2020 of him taking a shot at Kobe he deleted this tweet the next day on January 26, 2020 as news broke out that Kobe Bryant's plane crashed killing him and several others. This tweet was reposted by others on Twitter. Mocha grande @breeashh is one of many people who have this posted on her Twitter page.

There are many others on Twitter who constantly attack Michael Jordan, stating that because his stats of assists, rebounds aren't as high it means he's not as skilled. Yet they don't mention that his points per game are higher both in the regular season and in the playoffs. I would say that since MJ is already done as far as her career is concerned anyone can look up his statistics and accomplishments if they are willing to do the research like I did.

I ask the LeBron fanatics, what makes LeBron truly better than Michael Jordan to have him being the GOAT? What does LeBron do better? If LeBron is better, why does he need more top 5 to top 10 players with him to win championships? Did you know Scottie Pippen was not a top 5 player in the NBA when he played with Michael Jordan?

I don't want you to think I'm taking shots at Nick Wright, Shannon Sharpe, or Colin Cowherd. I really enjoy watching these guys as they talk about different sports and topics. What I want is for them to understand that they don't need to push the LeBron James as the GOAT every single day and in every segment. It gets old and it makes every day seem like a rerun rather than it being a live new segment. I believe what Fox Sports FS1 should do is have the GOAT debate only once a year at the end of the basketball Season. The GOAT debate does not need to be in every show or have their hosts claiming it in every segment.

The media members I listed use the arguments to support LeBron James by bringing up the arguments I have gone over. What should happen is this. Let's say Nick Wright wants to have a GOAT debate on his show, First Things First. If he does, all he has to do is let his network know in advance. Then have someone who is very knowledgeable of both players go on the show. I believe Chris Broussard and Skip Bayless have great points. Or maybe get permission to bring on Max Kellerman and Stephen A. Smith for a special episode (ESPN cross over with FS1) and have the debates. Many of these guys were covering the NBA and Michael Jordan. They have also watched and covered LeBron James. They can bring more details than I know. They can share possibly more facts. I would love to see if Nick Brings up the 1-9 first round record, to have his opposition challenge it by also sharing LeBron's early career as well. If opposition is a topic, bring up not just LeBron facing the Gold State Warriors, the warriors have only been a factor for five seasons of his 17 year career. This team has faced him four times in the championship. It has not been a factor for him for most of his career. Jordan had Milwaukee., Boston and Detroit, all of which had some great players that I mentioned in arguments 1 and 2. Two of those teams had four Hall of Fame players on their teams. This doesn't include me talking about the west where the LA Lakers had some other all time greats. Nick likes to water down the talent in LA, but they were still a great team. They were still going to the championship and were contenders through all of the 1980's and into the 1990/91 season. Have it where people are shown both sides of every argument. Include the points that I have brought up in this book. Maybe just maybe we will for once see a great GOAT debate on TV.

What I have seen is not great GOAT debates. Instead they have gotten worst over the past year. On First Things First I see Nick Wright get more and more emotional over these debates. His face gets all red and he constantly interrupts the guests and is disrespectful. He is shaking his head and making noises like grunt sounds that are just annoying. It's not even a debate anymore when he's on the show. His analytics are selected so it shows LeBron but most of the analytics will point to Jordan as the GOAT. Refer to the Analytics section of my GOAT arguments.

The fans in the live chats go off of these poorly made arguments that First Things First, Undisputed, The Herd and the various radio shows that Fox Sports has. Nick Wright was saying how Jordan didn't dominate and everyone won around him, so unless he is blind there are several HOF players and All Stars that have won while LeBron has been playing. It is good that there are knowledgeable and creditable hosts like Chris Broussard that can list the various players that Jordan has beaten during these shows. In LeBron's career more players have won a championship, but we don't bring that up every time a GOAT debate occurs. Jordan and LeBron are mainly compared on the main Analytics which include Points, Rebounds and Assists. These are to help the LeBron's case. But what should be compared is what these players do on both sides of the ball? OR shouldn't we compare more of the stats as per game instead of career totals? It should be obvious that when a player is playing the game longer, that that same player will get more accumulated stats?

My Analysis

All of the players I have mentioned have done incredible things in the game of Basketball. Each one has done something no one else has ever done in the sport. The sport today allows players to break some of these records once thought to be untouchable. If the game was more physical I wonder if players like LeBron would still have this longevity? That's something we will never know. I am someone who loves defense, and I appreciate the players who show consistency on defense when playing the game. Once defense is included that narrative no longer supports LeBron, why? It's because during his career, he has not been as efficient on the defensive side of the ball. While he does get 0.1 more blocks per game than Jordan, that stat is misconstrued that he's a better defender. If he was a better defender it would be more widely accepted by players and the media. I do see Colin Cowherd, Shannon Sharpe and Nick Wright all use that LeBron can guard every position, hence he is a better defender. According to NAB stats, players who played more than 15 minutes per game, LeBron James has one of the worst defensive ratings with 112.9. When Michael Jordan played, he leading in the player efficiency rating (29.4), win shares (20.4) and was ninth in defensive rating (99.6) according to the Bleacher Report. Just Because LeBron can guard multiple positions doesn't mean he's a better defender.

Fans also love to talk about the finals and play off records which is the most annoying argument because they pick and choose which record has more value. The YouTube channel Danger Productions goes over this subject of players losing a championship. I'm paraphrasing, If you ever talk to a fan about their team losing a championship, that fan will be sad, mad, disappointed and sometimes shocked. Players these emotions are felt even more. Some players never recover from a championship loss.

It is ridiculous to say getting to the championship and losing is better that losing prior. Unfortunately that is not true at all. As a player it is better to lose before the championship. It's easier to recover from an earlier loss than it is to recover from a championship loss. To give an argument that 6 losses is better than 0 losses is idiotic. LeBron is 4-6 in the championship. Jordan is 6-0. It will take LeBron at least double the appearances in the finals to possibly get 6 championships compared to Jordan. That does not say he is a better player. It just says he had been on enough teams that helped him get to the championship. During the 2019/20 season Anthony Davis lead the L.A. Lakers in every statistical category except assists. Yet he did not receive one MVP vote. LeBron felt he should have received more than 16 votes. Those 16 votes were biased because if he wasn't the best player that season on his own team, how does he get those votes? Yet the LeBron fanatics will say to this day LeBron has always been the best player on every team he's ever been on. I guess they don't count LeBron's first year in Miami when Dwayne Wade was the best player on the team, or LeBron's second year with the Lakers when Anthony Davis was the best player on the team.

The truth is no matter what facts myself or other media members bring, the LeBron fanatics will not listen to an argument we make. I have shown how other players are brought into the conversation when we look at other goat criteria. Yet unless it fits the LeBron narrative the fans will just continue to be disrespectful to all NBA players, and this includes Michael Jeffery Jordan.

Can LeBron become the GOAT?

He will be in the conversation for many years, even after he retires. He can become the first player to be playing in the league at the same time his son starts making it into the NBA. LeBron will achieve many great things in the league and will continue to break records. So he will build up his resume to keep him in the conversation. As this is a debate, the truth is I am telling you each players statistics, career accomplishments, what I think about each player and how I rank them. I don't know if you agree with my takes or not. When it comes to this topic of who the greatest player of all time is, it's really the opinion of the individual. As the years go by, this notion of Michael Jordan being the GOAT can change. It's based on perception. Chris Broussard once said that in the next twenty years or so the Michael Jordan supporters will no longer be in the media, it will then be the millennial's. This means that they will control the narrative and LeBron as the GOAT will be pushed more and it might be more widely accepted by the masses by that time. The GOAT debate is all based on each individual person's opinions.

Why do I think LeBron James could be considered the GOAT? LeBron James statistics are the things that I believe help his case in the GOAT debate. He is the only player to have over 30,000 points, 8,000 Rebounds and 8,000 Assists. He has done many incredible things in his career, and it's astonishing to see him break all of these statistical records every single season in the NBA. As I stated with Michael Jordan, Both players have needed players around them to win. This isn't something that should surprise anyone, because this is a team sport. LeBron also has the argument that he has been to the finals over 50% of his career. That accomplishment is rarely seen. Bill Russell is the only other player where he was in the championship almost every season of his career. LeBron may not win finals MVP every time he's in the championship but to make it there is something all players dream of.

Why I think LeBron James is not the goat? For me to place a player as the greatest of all time, I have really high expectations. I think that not only should a player dominate on offense, but defense as well. LeBron has only been dominating on the offensive side of the ball; however, he has underachieved in the defensive side. His lack of Defensive Player of the Year, Losing championships and not getting finals MVP in every Final's he's in is hard for me to over look. I can forget the meltdown in 2011, that's not something I concentrate on. To say he never has help is such a major lie; he's had some of the best teammates in the NBA. For his statistical dominance, like Wilt Chamberlain, he has underachieved and has not won as often as he should have. Rob Parker of FS1 has pointed out that LeBron James six finals losses also is the most any former MVP has had. This to me cannot be dismissed, losing matters. I also cannot say that if he gets 6 or more championship that he can pass Michael Jordan. No matter how many championships he has, he didn't do it better than Michael Jordan. It would take as I said earlier that he would have to be in at least double the championships to maybe tie Michael Jordan in titles. To make double the appearances and not have Jordan beat in titles does not place him as being better. The all time greats are said to be able to will their teams to victory, that they overcame the odds. This has never been said about LeBron James. He instead forms teams with other players and if things don't go his way, he leaves.

The Goat Summary

So here's a summary.

Greatest Passer: Irvine Magic Johnson

Greatest Winner: Bill Russell

Greatest Individual stats: LeBron James

Greatest Rebounder: Bill Russell

Greatest Single game scorer: Wilt Chamberlain (100 points)

Greatest Finals scorer: Michael Jordan.

Greatest Clutch Moment: Michael Jordan.

Greatest Defender: Michael Jordan.

Greatest winner as a Rookie: Irvine Magic Johnson.

Most MVP's: Kareem Abdul Jabbar (6)

Most Finals MVPs: Michael Jordan (6)

Defensive Player of the Year winners: Michael Jordan (1)

Scoring Titles: Michael Jordan (10).

All Star Selections: Kareem (19).

All Star MVP's: Kobe Bryant (4)

Triple Doubles-   Magic Johnson(30)

Who Is The Goat?

Answer: MICHAEL JORDAN

And here's why...

Remember how I said I would wait on putting his career into context. It is for this reason. He has the most complete resume for the GOAT compared to all of the other players, including this generation's greatest player LeBron James. Ultimately it comes down to overall career dominance, winning and being able to play basketball as a whole. LeBron fans dismiss the defensive side of basketball, only praising the triple doubles that we have come to expect from LeBron in the regular season and in the playoffs. Jordan was able to get triple doubles, but he didn't need to do it, instead he kept to his role of a shooting guard. Jordan was an offensive threat and he holds the finals records for most points scored in multiple finals and winning. Look at the Michael Jordan section where I talk about his averages. He was a known assassin and his killer instinct was shown on the court. He made shots that would make you think you are watching a movie or playing a video game. He defied gravity and jumping from the free throw line to slam the ball is one of the most iconic moments in all of the NBA.

The majority of the *Analytics* points to Michael Jordan as the better player. The Value over Replacement, Box Plus/Minus, Player Efficiency Rating and usage percentage favor Michael Jordan over LeBron.

Using Jalen Rose's criteria mentioned towards the beginning, He won 10 *scoring titles*, he has 5 regular season *MVP awards*, Six *championships*, Six *Finals MVP* awards, and got one Defensive Player of the Year award. With my added criteria he has 14 *All Stars*, 3 *All Star MVP* awards, one of which included his last year winning a championship in 1998. . Jordan won *Rookie of the Year* in the 1984/85 season. Jordan led the league in steals for three straight years, he was a 9 time All Defensive First team. He won the regular season MVP and *Defensive Player of the Year* in the same season 1988 and was the first player ever in the sport to accomplish this feat. He has two Gold medals, one he won as a Rookie, and the other on the 1992 Dream Team, which by many is believed to be the best gold medal team ever assembled by the United States. That 1992 Dream team is also now in the Hall of Fame. Jordan is also the oldest player to make the all star game.

EPSN show First Take the moderator Molly Qerim has pointed out that Michael Jordan was still a good player during his years as a Wizard, after all he was still an All Star when he was playing with the Wizards. So while I didn't go much into his Wizards career, he was still a top player. His team just wasn't that good. You can see people like Chris Broussard talk about "You just don't know how good Michael Jordan was with the Wizards." You can find it on YouTube. LeBron fans try to use the tail end of Jordan's career to disqualify him as the GOAT, but despite what they say it doesn't change the fact that even then at age 40 he was still one of the best players in the league. The Wizard years don't take away from him being the GOAT.

In NBA Rankings, Bleacher Report has placed The Bulls team from 1996 as the second greatest team ever. This team is lead by Michael Jordan and many argue that the 96' Bulls team is the greatest team ever. President Barack Obama has said after the 2016 Cleveland Cavaliers championship, when they were at the White House, that the Cav's beating the Warriors solidified the 96 Bull's team as the Greatest team ever. Do you believe Barack Obama? Michael Jordan has also been at the top of the Bleacher report list at the #1 Spot for the greatest player of all time. Michael Jordan also helped the laughable Bulls to be one of the most dominate Dynasties ever in all of sports. As of today the Chicago Bulls are the only franchise to have no finals losses and multiple appearances in the NBA Finals. This dynasty and franchise again was lead by Michael Jordan. During the 90's While Jordan was playing, the Bulls simply didn't lose. They won Six championships in 8 years. In that time span Jordan missed the 1993/94 season for baseball and re-entered the NBA in the 1994/95 season where he only played 18 regular season games. There are those who try to use that against him but it doesn't hide the fact that in every full season Jordan played from 1990/91 season to the 1997/98 season Jordan and the Bulls did not lose. He dominated the League and no one could beat him. He made many teams not seem as good simply because they played during the Michael Jordan era. For years, there have been many polls conducted by several media outlets have nearly 70 percent or more on players and fans placing Jordan as the GOAT.

"Michael Jordan, basketball's greatest player ever, was among a class of five enshrined in the Naismith Memorial Basketball Hall of Fame on Sept. 11, **2009**. The Class of **2009**, which also included Jerry Sloan, John Stockton, C. Vivian Stringer and David Robinson, was inducted during festivities in Springfield, MA." According to NBA.com on him being inducted into the Hall of Fame.

Michael Jordan also has a statue of him located in front of the United Center, the Chicago Bulls stadium. The statue according to UnitedCenter.com has the statue measuring at 12 feet tall, and weighing 2,000 pounds. This is a Bronze sculpture with a black granite base. This was created in 1994 to honor him and to retire his number 23.

He helped globalize the NBA, making it go from approximately 50 countries to over 200. He became a world icon and is known as the ultimate winner when it comes to being perfect in the championship. He changed how people dress and got a track and field Shoe Company become a fashionable accessory for people to wear. His shoes were even highlighted in the blockbuster movie He Got Game. He not only won 6 championships, but he never lost in any championship he was in during his professional career, this not only includes the finals, but the McDonalds Championship Series and two Olympics. Every championship he was in, he was the best player and got Finals MVP every time. Jordan is the most completed player and he showed it from the first day he played in the NBA to his final game in 2003. He never lost his drive and will to win in the game of basketball.

Michael Jordan is and remains the UNDISPUTED GREATEST OF ALL TIME in the game of basketball.

References

Rosters and Stats provided by basketballreference.com, NBA.com

Michael Jordan Rookie season provided by chicagobulls.com, NBA.com

Arguments: GOAT arguments topics provided from ESPN and Fox Sport Shows.

Accolades provided by LandofBasketball.com

The Last Dance Documentary (1998 Chicago Bulls)

HBO Documentary Bill Russell, My life my way.

Michael Jordan IMBD

LeBron James IMBD

BossHunting. *Michael Jordan Net Worth: How He Spends $2.7 Billion.* April 10, 2020. https://www.bosshunting.com.au/culture/michael-jordan-net-worth/

New York Times. Milwaukee Bucks Fined $50,000 for Tampering (With Their Own Player). Sept. 24, 2019. https://www.nytimes.com/2019/09/24/sports/milwaukee-bucks-tampering-giannis.html

The Spun. Chris Rosvoglou. *The 20 Hall Of Famers Michael Jordan Knocked Out Of The Playoffs.* May 19, 2020. https://thespun.com/nba/chicago-bulls/hall-of-famers-michael-jordan-knocked-out-of-the-playoffs

NBA official website, history of the Chicago Bulls, Michael Jordan. https://www.nba.com/bulls/history/players/michael-jordan

Fox Sports Radio Clay Travis- *The Hypocrisy of LeBron James Telling Daryl Morey to Shut Up & GM.* Premiered Oct 15, 2019. https://www.youtube.com/watch?v=yIzNMKoBF44

Michael Jordan's world. https://www.michaeljordansworld.com/stats_finals.htm

MSN Sporting News. *Michael Jordan vs. LeBron James: The key stats you need to know in the GOAT debate* Jordan Greer. 4/19/2020. https://www.msn.com/en-us/sports/nba/michael-jordan-vs-lebron-james-the-key-stats-you-need-to-know-in-the-goat-debate/ar-BB12STDB

Bleacher Report. *The Cult of Deficiency: A Look at ESPN's John Hollinger and His Flawed Rankings.* William Johnson. 4/12/2011. https://bleacherreport.com/articles/654735-the-cult-of-deficiency-a-look-at-espns-john-hollinger-and-his-flawed-rankings

Basketball Reference. Player Value over replacement https://www.basketball-reference.com/leaders/vorp_season.html

Basketball Reference. Player Efficiency rating. https://www.basketball-reference.com/leaders/per_career.html

Basketball Reference Box plus/minus https://www.basketball-reference.com/leaders/bpm career.html

Basketball Reference win shares https://www.basketball-reference.com/leaders/ws career.html

Basketball Reference True Shooting percentage https://www.basketball-reference.com/leaders/ts pct career.html

How They Play. Michael Jordan Versus LeBron James: Who Is the GOAT? Jesse Unk. 10/12/2020. https://howtheyplay.com/team-sports/Michael-Jordan-Versus-LeBron-James#:~:text=LeBron%20Is%20More%20Clutch%20than%20Jordan%20The%20statistics,each%20except%20for%20free%20throw%20percentage%20and%20turnovers.

EPSN The Jump. Is LeBron as clutch as Michael Jordan? 4/26/2018 https://www.bing.com/videos/search?q=more+clutch+stats+lebron+vs+jordan&docid=607994419832294228&mid=B8AD441A17CE54CBA7FEB8AD441A17CE54CBA7FE&view=detail&FORM=VIRE

ESPN Potential Game-Tying/Go-Ahead FG. 6/14/2018. https://twitter.com/espnstatsinfo/status/1007408491894624256

NBA Agent Calls out LeBron James, Rich Paul's Handling of Klutch Sports Athletes, Rob Goldberg, Bleacher Report. October 22, 20202. www.bleacherreport.com

Michael Jordan Statue, United Center. https://www.unitedcenter.com/venue/statues/

"A Betting Odds History of the 1990s Chicago Bulls Dynasty" Matt Moore, Action Network, May 6, 2020. https://www.actionnetwork.com/nba/betting-odds-history-1990s-chicago-bulls-dynasty-michael-jordan

"The Greatest Expectations." Zack Kram. The Ringer. May 11, 2020. https://www.theringer.com/nba/2020/5/11/21254188/title-expectations-michael-jordan-lebron-james

Printed in the United States
By Bookmasters